AWS Lambda Qui Guide

Learn how to build and deploy serverless applications on AWS

Markus Klems

BIRMINGHAM - MUMBAI

AWS Lambda Quick Start Guide

Commissioning Editor: Wilson D'souza
Acquisition Editor: Reshma Raman
Content Development Editor: Roshan Kumar
Technical Editor: Shweta Jadhav
Copy Editor: Safis Editing
Project Coordinator: Hardik Bhinde
Proofreader: Safis Editing
Indexer: Aishwarya Gangawane
Graphics: Jisha Chirayil
Production Coordinator: Deepika Naik

First published: June 2018

Production reference: 1290618

Published by Packt Publishing Ltd.
Livery Place
35 Livery Street
Birmingham
B3 2PB, UK.

ISBN 978-1-78934-019-8

www.packtpub.com

mapt.io

Mapt is an online digital library that gives you full access to over 5,000 books and videos, as well as industry leading tools to help you plan your personal development and advance your career. For more information, please visit our website.

Why subscribe?

- Spend less time learning and more time coding with practical eBooks and Videos from over 4,000 industry professionals
- Improve your learning with Skill Plans built especially for you
- Get a free eBook or video every month
- Mapt is fully searchable
- Copy and paste, print, and bookmark content

PacktPub.com

Did you know that Packt offers eBook versions of every book published, with PDF and ePub files available? You can upgrade to the eBook version at www.PacktPub.com and, as a print book customer, you are entitled to a discount on the eBook copy. Get in touch with us at service@packtpub.com for more details.

At www.PacktPub.com, you can also read a collection of free technical articles, sign up for a range of free newsletters, and receive exclusive discounts and offers on Packt books and eBooks.

Contributors

About the author

Markus Klems is a software development and system administration expert for scalable, high-availability, and high-performance software systems, such as big data, mobile, web application, and Software-as-a-Service systems. Within the framework of his research and development work at TU Berlin and Karlsruhe Institute of Technology (KIT), Markus has gained in-depth knowledge and experience of complex and large-scale IT systems. He has been working with Amazon Web Services (AWS) since 2008 and is particularly excited about serverless computing and serverless microservice architectures.

Packt is searching for authors like you

If you're interested in becoming an author for Packt, please visit `authors.packtpub.com` and apply today. We have worked with thousands of developers and tech professionals, just like you, to help them share their insight with the global tech community. You can make a general application, apply for a specific hot topic that we are recruiting an author for, or submit your own idea.

Table of Contents

Preface

Welcome to Learning AWS Lambda!

In this book, you will learn how to use Lambda, how to use it in combination with other AWS services, in particular API Gateway Service, but also services such as DynamoDB, which is the database as a service offering by Amazon that is also a pay-per-use utility-based, utility computing-based service, which works very well in the context of our serverless application architecture.

Also, we will look at other Amazon Web Services that work well alongside Lambda. In addition, you will learn how to use the serverless framework to build larger applications to structure your code, to autogenerate boilerplate code that you can use to get started quickly. In this video, we will explore Lambda and you will learn how to build scalable and cost-efficient applications that require nearly no operations once you have built and deployed your application.

So let's get started on this wonderful journey.

What this book covers

Chapter 1, *Getting Started with AWS*, gives you an introduction to the fundamental concepts of AWS and also explores the AWS web dashboard. You will also learn to create and test your first lambda function as well.

Chapter 2, *Exploring the Serverless Framework*, teaches you how to use the Serverless Framework to create and test Lambda functions and APIs. You will also try out different approaches for API testing, Lambda testing, and debugging.

Chapter 3, *Building a Serverless Application*, shows you how to build your first serverless application.

Chapter 4, *Programming AWS Lambda with Java*, focuses on how to program Lambda using Java. You will also learn how to use Eclipse with the AWS Toolkit plugin.

Chapter 5, *Programming AWS Lambda with Python*, features how to create Lambda functions from blueprints on the AWS Management Console using Python.

Chapter 6, *Programming AWS Lambda with C#*, showcases how to create C# Lambda functions and serverless projects with NET Core.

What you need for this book

The only prerequisite for this course is to have basic programming or scripting experience, which will facilitate the understanding of the examples quickly.

In terms of environment, you only need to download the virtual machine that contains the vulnerable target web application and the Python environment with all the necessary libraries. To run a virtual machine, you will need to install VirtualBox from www.virtualbox.org.

Who this book is for

This book is primarily for IT architects and developers who want to build scalable systems and deploy serverless applications with AWS Lambda. No prior knowledge of AWS is necessary.

To get the most out of this book

This book will give you the maximum benefit if you have some theoretical knowledge of AWS services. Additionally, install the following in your system:

- Java version 1.8
- Visual Studio 2015
- Python 2.7.15

Download the example code files

You can download the example code files for this book from your account at www.packtpub.com. If you purchased this book elsewhere, you can visit www.packtpub.com/support and register to have the files emailed directly to you.

You can download the code files by following these steps:

1. Log in or register at www.packtpub.com.
2. Select the **SUPPORT** tab.
3. Click on **Code Downloads & Errata**.
4. Enter the name of the book in the **Search** box and follow the onscreen instructions.

Once the file is downloaded, please make sure that you unzip or extract the folder using the latest version of:

- WinRAR/7-Zip for Windows
- Zipeg/iZip/UnRarX for Mac
- 7-Zip/PeaZip for Linux

The code bundle for the book is also hosted on GitHub at `https://github.com/PacktPublishing/AWS-Lambda-Quick-Start-Guide`. In case there's an update to the code, it will be updated on the existing GitHub repository.

We also have other code bundles from our rich catalog of books and videos available at `https://github.com/PacktPublishing/`. Check them out!

Download the color images

We also provide a PDF file that has color images of the screenshots/diagrams used in this book. You can download it here: `https://www.packtpub.com/sites/default/files/downloads/AWSLambdaQuickStartGuide_ColorImages.pdf`.

Conventions used

There are a number of text conventions used throughout this book.

`CodeInText`: Indicates code words in text, database table names, folder names, filenames, file extensions, pathnames, dummy URLs, user input, and Twitter handles. Here is an example: "Mount the downloaded `WebStorm-10*.dmg` disk image file as another disk in your system."

A block of code is set as follows:

```
service: blog
provider:
  name: aws
  runtime: nodejs4.3
  stage: dev
  region: eu-central-1
```

Any command-line input or output is written as follows:

```
sls create -t aws-nodejs -n blog
```

Bold: Indicates a new term, an important word, or words that you see on screen. For example, words in menus or dialog boxes appear in the text like this. Here is an example: "Select **System info** from the **Administration** panel."

Warnings or important notes appear like this.

Tips and tricks appear like this.

Get in touch

Feedback from our readers is always welcome.

General feedback: Email feedback@packtpub.com and mention the book title in the subject of your message. If you have questions about any aspect of this book, please email us at questions@packtpub.com.

Errata: Although we have taken every care to ensure the accuracy of our content, mistakes do happen. If you have found a mistake in this book, we would be grateful if you would report this to us. Please visit www.packtpub.com/submit-errata, selecting your book, clicking on the Errata Submission Form link, and entering the details.

Piracy: If you come across any illegal copies of our works in any form on the internet, we would be grateful if you would provide us with the location address or website name. Please contact us at copyright@packtpub.com with a link to the material.

If you are interested in becoming an author: If there is a topic that you have expertise in and you are interested in either writing or contributing to a book, please visit authors.packtpub.com.

Reviews

Please leave a review. Once you have read and used this book, why not leave a review on the site that you purchased it from? Potential readers can then see and use your unbiased opinion to make purchase decisions, we at Packt can understand what you think about our products, and our authors can see your feedback on their book. Thank you!

For more information about Packt, please visit `packtpub.com`.

Bibliography

The material in this book has been selected from the content of Packt's video *Learning AWS Lambda* by Markus Klems to provide a specific focus on learning to build and deploy serverless apps on AWS.

Getting Started with AWS 1

Amazon Web Services (**AWS**) is a collection of web services that together make up a cloud computing platform that can help make an organization more efficient. It offers a broad set of global computing, storage, database, analytic, application, and deployment services. AWS is very beneficial as it is highly flexible and very easy to use. It is also very cost-effective and reliable, with high performance and scalability.

In this chapter, we are going to take a look at fundamental AWS concepts, such as cloud service usage and pricing models. We will explore the AWS web dashboard, the so-called **Management Console**. On the **Management Console**, we will take our first steps with Lambda and the API Gateway Service.

Now, we are going to have a look at the following topics:

- Introduction to the fundamental concepts of AWS
- AWS account walkthrough
- AWS Lambda
- AWS API Gateway

Installation and setup guide

Before going any further into how to use AWS, let's first create and set up an AWS account. This is a prerequisite for getting started with programming AWS Lambda. Here, I'm going to show you how to sign up for an AWS account and then I will show you how to create a special IAM user with administrator access permissions. After that, I'll show you how to set up a local development environment with AWS credentials. So let's dive in:

1. First, open the web browser on the main website of Amazon Web Services, `https://aws.amazon.com/`
2. Click on the **Create an AWS Account** button to create a new AWS account
3. Select the **I am a new user** radio button and enter your email address
4. Then, fill out the rest of the information and go through the sign-up process:

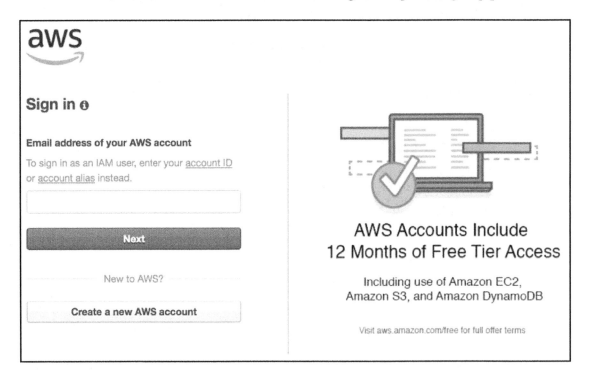

Once the account has been created, sign in to the AWS **Management Console**. More information on the console will be provided later on. For now, click **Services** in the drop-down menu and search for IAM. Click on **IAM** to navigate to the **Identity and Access Management** dashboard. Here, I am going to show you how to create a special IAM user that has certain permissions to use AWS services on my behalf. This is a good security practice. You shouldn't use your root account credentials for programmatically accessing Amazon Web Services. It could create problems for you—for example, you could accidentally publish your AWS credentials on GitHub or somewhere else where other people can see them, and using these details, they could then use your AWS services. If this happens to you, it's pretty easy to use IAM to simply delete your user and revoke these permissions:

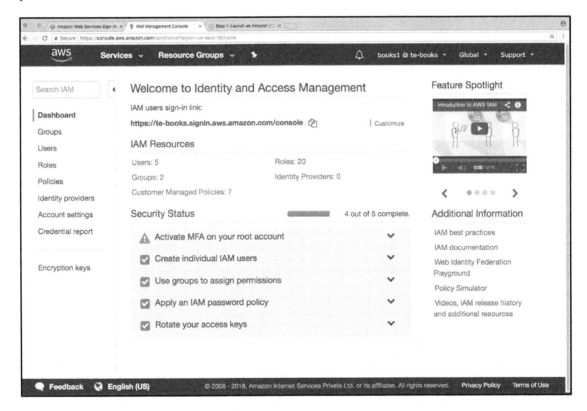

In this tutorial, I'm going to create a group and an IAM user to perform the exercises. After we are done with the tutorial, you can simply delete the user and the group.

Let's start by creating an IAM group. Set up a group name. For this tutorial, I am naming the group `learninggroup`. For simplicity, what I'm going to do is give my group administrator access. If you're more paranoid, you can restrict this further, but then you might have to deal with a bit more hassle. I think for the purposes of this tutorial, and assuming that you will delete this group and the user later on, it's fine to go with administrator access. Click on **Next Step and Create Group**.

Now I'm going to create a new user. Click on **Users** | **Add User**. Here, I will give my user the name `learninglambda`, and I'm going to select the programmatic access checkbox. This will create an access key ID and a secret access key so that you can programmatically use Amazon Web Services:

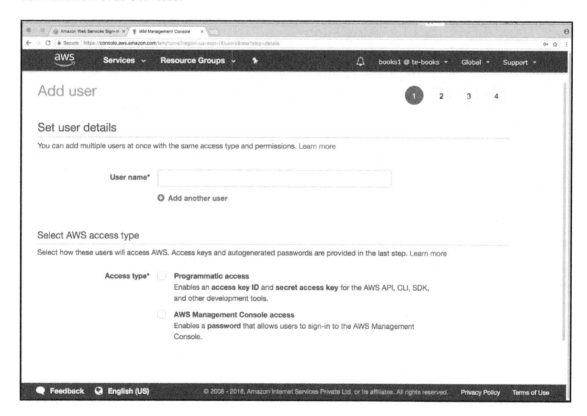

In the next step, I will show you how to set up your local development environment with the access key ID and the secret access key ID so that you can use AWS from within IDEs, such as Eclipse or Visual Studio, or through development frameworks, such as the Serverless framework. If you want, you could also give your new IAM user AWS Management Console access. Click on **Next Permissions**. I added my IAM user to the `learninggroup` and now I'm going to create the user. Once the user has been created, you will be provided with the access key ID and the secret access key ID. Copy both of them into a blank text file as you will need them for the next step. Copy both of them into a text editor:

```
AKIAIWRW3LZDPQIY3TPQ
v9kIjVVCd0pDWTB0LJDKtVi3+MVlYhkDlyBF79z7
```

Now, I'm going to show you how to set up your local development environment so that you can programmatically access AWS services from within your local development environment. This is used by a number of IDEs, such as Eclipse or Visual Studio, and other development frameworks, such as the Serverless framework. I'm going to show you how to do this for macOS. It works in a similar way for Linux.

So the first thing that we need to do is create a hidden directory named `AWS` in your home folder. I created a hidden directory, and now in that directory I will create a file named `credentials`. In that file, I'm going copy my access key and my secret access key in the following format. What this does is specify the IAM profile that I want to use:

```
mkdir ~/.aws
touch ~/.aws/credentials
```

This is the default IAM profile that my IDE or development framework is going to use with the following access key ID and secret access key credentials. After you have entered the content into your `credentials` file, it should look like the following:

```
[default]
aws_access_key_id=AKIAISSXZB2PNT6VVG3Q
aws_secret_access_key=ybv3rDoNNJDdbF019XWxVaHv0t8bYF5p0hU5g
```

You need to set up your own access key ID and secret access key, because the credentials that we have been using will soon not exist anymore:

```
cat ~/.aws/credentials
```

Now I am going to explain how to set up your AWS credentials file on your operating system.

Set up your local development PC/laptop with AWS credentials

If you are using Linux or macOS, you should create a hidden directory, `.aws`, in your home folder. If you're using Windows, you should create a hidden AWS directory in your user's profile directory. Then you copy the content, your access key ID, and the secret access key.

Installing the Serverless framework

To install the Serverless framework, you basically need to do the following:

- You need to install Node.js. When you install Node.js, the Node package manager will be installed.
- Then you can use npm, the Node package manager, to install the Serverless framework by typing `npm install -g`. This will initiate a global installation so you can launch the serverless command from anywhere on Terminal. Type `npm install -g serverless` into Terminal to install the Serverless framework using the node package manager.

You can also follow the guide at `https://serverless.com/framework/docs/providers/aws/guide/installation/`.

Introduction to AWS

Let's move on to the first official section of this chapter, which gives you an introduction to AWS. In this section, we are going to take a look at Lambda usage and pay-per-use pricing, and also where to find documentation and other developer resources:

1. Let's go to the home page for `aws.Amazon.com/lambda`, as shown in the following screenshot:

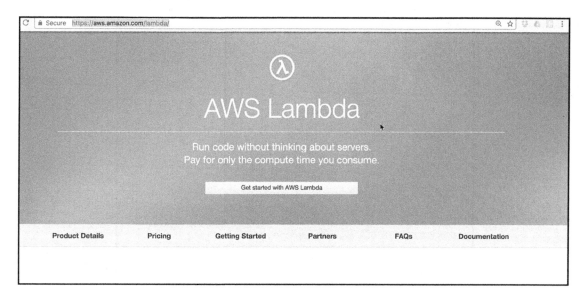

2. Head over to the **Documentation** page. The **Documentation** page gives you links to many useful resources, such as SDKs and tools. But, for now, let's take a look at the Developer Guide.
3. The Developer Guide gives us a lot of useful background information on how Lambda works.

4. Click on the section called **Building Applications with AWS** and click on the **Event Source Mapping**:

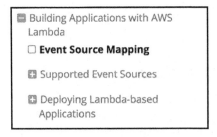

5. Scroll down a bit and you will be able to see an example of how we can use Lambda, shown in the following screenshot:

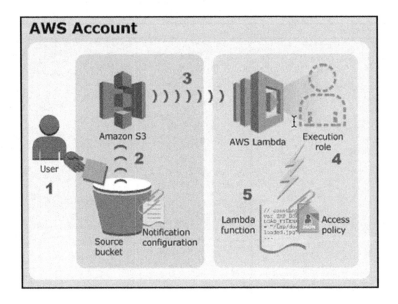

In this example, Amazon S3 pushes events and invokes a Lambda function. **Amazon S3** (or **Amazon Simple Storage Service**) is a scalable web service for storing and retrieving large amounts of data. In this example, we have a user who uploads a file into an Amazon S3 bucket. This triggers an object-created event. The object-created event is detected by Amazon S3, which triggers S3 to invoke our Lambda function. The Lambda function is associated with an execution role. The execution role gives our set certain permissions. So, in this scenario, Amazon S3 needs to have permissions to invoke our Lambda function, otherwise any other service would be able to invoke our Lambda function, which we want to avoid. So, if these permissions are given, our Lambda function is invoked with the event data from our Amazon S3 service invocation. This is also referred to as the push event model, but there's another way to use AWS Lambda. Let's scroll down a little bit to the next example:

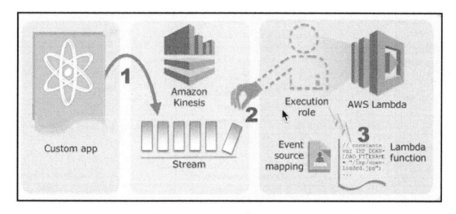

Here, we have a stream-based service. In this example, Lambda pulls events from an Amazon Kinesis stream and invokes the Lambda function. On the left-hand side, you can see a custom application that writes data on a Kinesis stream. On the right-hand side, our Lambda function continuously picks up pieces or records from this stream. Again, we have an execution role associated with our Lambda function, but in this case it works the other way around. In this case, we need to give our Lambda function permission to access the Kinesis stream because here we are in the so-called pull event model. Whenever we pick up a new record, the Lambda function is executed.

Cloud service pricing

Now let's take a quick look at cloud service pricing. Cloud services work quite differently from traditional web hosting, and this also applies to pricing. With the traditional web hoster, you typically sign up for a long-term contract, maybe one year or two years, and you pay for the resources whether you use them or not. With cloud services, this works quite differently. With cloud services, you only pay for the resources that you actually use with very fine granularity. The downside of this is that the pricing model becomes a bit more complicated:

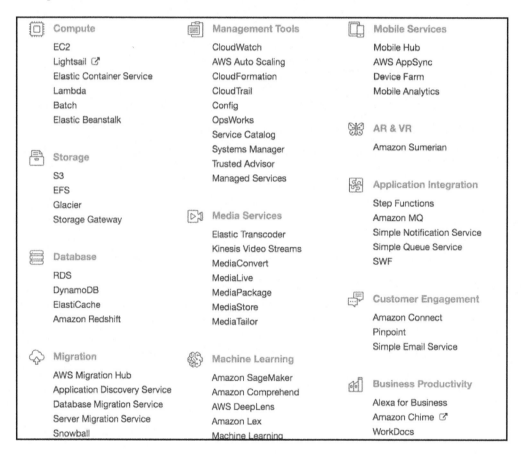

As you can see in the preceding screenshot, each Amazon web service has its individual pricing model. Typically, it breaks down into charges for the compute capacity, storage capacity, and data transfer that you use.

Let's take a closer look at the pricing model of AWS Lambda. The pricing model breaks down into two parts:

- First, you pay for requests, which is actually quite cheap. It's only 20 cents for 1 million requests.
- The other thing that you pay for is duration, which is the time that your Lambda function runs for. This time period is rounded up to the nearest 100 milliseconds. So, if you have a short-running Lambda function that only runs for 50 milliseconds, you pay for 100. If you have a Lambda function that runs for 910 milliseconds, you pay for 1 full second. You also have to pay for the amount of memory that you allocate to your function. You can configure your Lambda function with different levels of memory. You then get charged this fixed price, price constant, for every gigabyte-second that you use.

Let's take a quick look at a sample calculation. When you scroll further down in the page, you will see different pricing examples. Let's have a look at the first pricing example.

Pricing example

In this example, you will configure your Lambda function with half a gigabyte of memory. We will assume that the Lambda function is called 3 million times within one month. Each Lambda function, we will assume, runs for one second. With this in mind, our monthly compute charges would be calculated as follows:

Monthly compute charges

The monthly compute price is $0.00001667 per GB-s and the free tier provides 400,000 GB-s.

Total compute (seconds) = 3M * (1s) = 3,000,000 seconds

Total compute (GB-s) = 3,000,000 * 512MB/1024 = 1,500,000 GB-s

Total compute – Free tier compute = Monthly billable compute GB- s

1,500,000 GB-s – 400,000 free tier GB-s = 1,100,000 GB-s

Monthly compute charges = 1,100,000 * $0.00001667 = $18.34

Given these details, we need to calculate the total amount of time that our Lambda function is running for: 3 million invocations X one second per invocation is equal to 3 million seconds. Then we calculate the compute capacity that is used during these invocations. We use Lambda functions for 3 million seconds, and each Lambda function is allocated with half a gigabyte of memory, so we use 1.5 gigabyte-seconds. However, Lambda comes with a free tier, so up to a certain level you get compute capacity and requests for free. So if you deduct these from your calculation, then you end up with 1.1 gigabyte-seconds. To calculate this, you multiply that with your fixed price constant and you end up with roughly 18 dollars per month:

Monthly request charges

The monthly request price is $0.20 per 1 million requests and the free tier provides 1M requests per month.

Total requests – Free tier requests – Monthly billable requests

3M requests – 1M free tier requests = 2M Monthly billable requests

Monthly request charges = 2M * $0.2/M = $0.40

You must also pay for request charges. However, this only costs 20 cents per million requests, and the first million requests are free, so you only have to pay for 2 million requests, which in other words will cost you only 40 cents.

So your final calculation for the monthly charges will amount to roughly 18-19 dollars per month (both the compute and request charges).

The next section is about the AWS web dashboard, the so-called Management Console. So let's dive into that!

AWS Management Console

After reading the previous section, you will be familiar with Lambda usage and pricing models. Now we are going to explore the AWS Management Console.

In this section, we are going to take a look at how to navigate the **Management Console**, how to switch between services, and what Amazon Web Service regions are. Get onto the landing page of AWS, `aws.amazon.com`. Sign in to the **Management Console** by clicking on the button in the upper-right corner. Once signed in, you will see a navigation bar on the top. On the left-hand side, there's a **Services** dropdown. You can see all the Amazon Web Services that are available to us, as shown in the following screenshot:

These services are all clustered by service category; for example, compute services such as **EC2-Lambda** are also in this category. We also have storage services, such as **S3**, the simple storage service. We also have database services, such as **DynamoDB**, a database service that we will use later. Finally, there are also application services, such as API Gateway. You can also pin certain services to your navigation bar to access them more quickly. Click on the little pin button and you can drag down a service or drag up a certain service. Click the little pin button again; now it's stuck to your navigation bar.

Regions

One concept that is important to know about is the concept of regions. I'm currently in the **North Virginia**, or **US East 1**, region. This is the default region for all Amazon Web Services. If I click on this drop-down menu, I can see other regions, such as **Ohio**, **Northern California**, **Ireland**, **Frankfurt**, and so on. Each region corresponds to an Amazon Web Services data center, and most services are specific to a certain region, so if you create resources, they are bound to the particular region that they were created in. If you switch region, you won't see resources that you created in another region. Moreover, not all services are available in all regions. If we click, for example, on Lambda, then we can see that Lambda is available in **Northern Virginia**, but it is not available in **Canada Central**, in **Asia Pacific Mumbai**, or in **South America**, at least not at the time of writing. So it will typically take some time before all regions catch up and support all services. In this tutorial, I will use the **EU Frankfurt** region, and I would advise that you use the same region so that what I show you is consistent with what you are doing.

So if you use a service in a certain region, it typically has a region-specific endpoint. You can find more information about regions and endpoints at
`docs.aws.amazon.com/general/latest/gr/rande.html`.

The following screenshot shows regions where Lambda is available:

Region Name	Region	Endpoint	Protocol
AWS Lambda			
US East (N. Virginia)	us-east-1	lambda.us-east-1.amazonaws.com	HTTPS
US East (Ohio)	us-east-2	lambda.us-east-2.amazonaws.com	HTTPS
US West (N. California)	us-west-1	lambda.us-west-1.amazonaws.com	HTTPS
US West (Oregon)	us-west-2	lambda.us-west-2.amazonaws.com	HTTPS
Asia Pacific (Seoul)	ap-northeast-2	lambda.ap-northeast-2.amazonaws.com	HTTPS
Asia Pacific (Singapore)	ap-southeast-1	lambda.ap-southeast-1.amazonaws.com	HTTPS
Asia Pacific (Sydney)	ap-southeast-2	lambda.ap-southeast-2.amazonaws.com	HTTPS
Asia Pacific (Tokyo)	ap-northeast-1	lambda.ap-northeast-1.amazonaws.com	HTTPS
EU (Frankfurt)	eu-central-1	lambda.eu-central-1.amazonaws.com	HTTPS
EU (Ireland)	eu-west-1	lambda.eu-west-1.amazonaws.com	HTTPS
EU (London)	eu-west-2	lambda.eu-west-2.amazonaws.com	HTTPS

In the next section, we are going to create our first Lambda function. Let's get on with that!

AWS Lambda

In the previous section, we learned about the Amazon Web Service Management Console. Now we will look into AWS Lambda. Here, we are going to take a look at the Lambda web dashboard, the Lambda function blueprints, how to configure and deploy the Lambda function, and how to test it—all from the **Management Console**. So let's head over to the Lambda service.

 To learn how to access the Lambda service, read the AWS Management Console section.

Once you are in your Lambda web dashboard, click on the blue **Get Started Now** button to create your first function.

You can select from a number of blueprints, which give you Lambda functions with a little bit of dummy code. You can filter by runtime, and since this is volume one, we want to use Node.js. So click on **Node.js 4.3**:

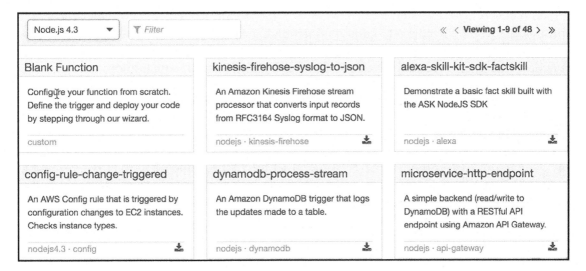

Let's use the Blank Function blueprint. If I want, I can create a trigger that triggers my Lambda function. There are different kinds of triggers, but for the first exercise, let's not select any trigger. Let's leave it empty and just click on the **Next** button.

Now we need to enter some configuration information for our function, such as a function name:

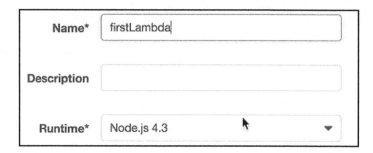

The runtime is correct, so we will scroll down a little bit. Here you can see that I have a function handler, as shown in the highlighted portion in the following code:

```
exports.handler = (event, context, callback) => {
    // TODO implement
    callback(null, 'Hello from Lamda');
};
```

This function will be assigned to the `exports.handler` property, which is then exported through the Node.js export. My Lambda function handler takes up to three arguments. The last argument, the callback, is optional. The first argument is my event, so my Lambda function; is triggered through an event. The caller of my Lambda function can pass in information. For example, if an S3 object-created event invokes my Lambda function, I can retrieve object metadata. If an HTTP request invokes my Lambda function, I can retrieve, for example, a JSON body from the HTTP event. The second object is the context of my Lambda function, I can access runtime information through this context object. Last but not least, the optional callback function is the typical Node.js error-first callback function. I can invoke it in this case without an error, so I will set the first parameter, or the first argument, to null. I also set the result, the second argument, to Hello from Lambda. So the caller will retrieve the message Hello from Lambda when the Lambda function is invoked.

What we also need to do is set the right permissions for the Lambda function. So scroll down to the Lambda function handler and role. Click on the **Role** dropdown, and create a custom role. Select `lambda_basic_execution` in the IAM Role dropdown and click on Allow. This will set the role to Lambda basic execution, as shown in the following screenshot:

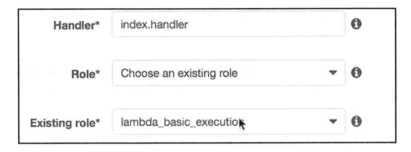

You can even configure the amount of memory that you want to use in your Lambda function by scrolling down. Remember, the more memory you give it, the faster it executes, but the more you have to pay. Let's stick to the smallest amount, 128 megabytes. You can also specify a timeout so that if the Lambda function doesn't terminate within this amount of time, then it times out. Let's leave it at the default of three seconds.

Scroll down and click on the **Next** button. Have a look at the settings, scroll down, and click on **Create Function**. You will be able to obtain similar details to those shown in the following screenshot:

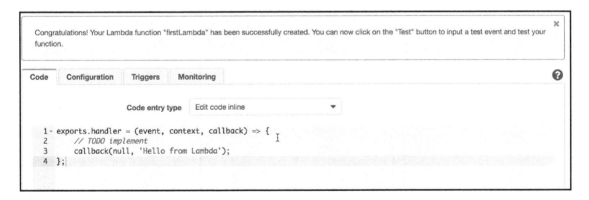

Congrats! You have created your first Lambda function! Let's test it.

Click on the **Test** button and this will execute the test that results in Lambda saying **Hello**.

You can also configure your test event in this way and give it sample event data. Since I don't use the event in my simple Lambda function at all, it doesn't matter what is pasted—simply click Save and Test.

AWS API Gateway

In the previous section, we created our first Lambda function. Now let's explore the API Gateway Service. Let's take a look at the API Gateway Service web dashboard. We will use it to create a new API and then connect that API to our Lambda function. Last but not least, we will test our API, and through our API, we will invoke the Lambda function. So let's start.

Log in to the Management Console in the Frankfurt region where you can create your first Lambda function. Now let's go to the API Gateway Service. If you don't have an API gateway, click on Let's Get Started. Amazon might ask you to import an API. Import it, and once done, you will be able to see a reference API that can be used to learn more about APIs, but it will be a bit too complex for our first use case. So, let's create a simpler API by clicking on the Create API button. Create a new API and give it the name `FirstAPI`. After that, click on `Create API`.

So now I have an API, and it can configure a couple of things, but for now, let's just create a resource that can be found in the Actions button, as shown in the following screenshot:

I will take a REST resource and name it foo. It will get the resource path foo. After this, I will click on Create Resource. A resource alone is not enough; I also need a method. So let's click on `Create` method and select an HTTP `GET` method, as seen in the following screenshot:

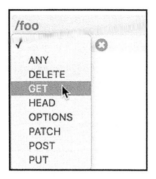

Click on the little checkmark. Et voila! We have a simple API with one resource, `foo`, and a `GET` method:

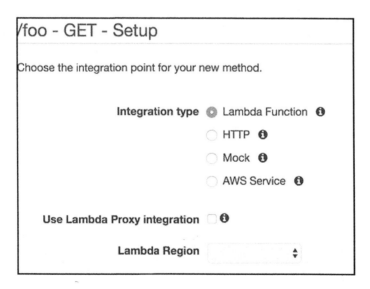

Now we can integrate it with different kinds of services. We want to integrate it with our Lambda function, so the first radio button is correct. We select the region. In our current example, we are in the Frankfurt region and our Lambda function is also in the Frankfurt region, so select `eu-central-1`, which is the Frankfurt region, and then type in the Lambda function name. I gave it the name `firstLambda`. Click on **Save**.

Now the API gateway will ask you if you give the API gateway permission to invoke your Lambda function:

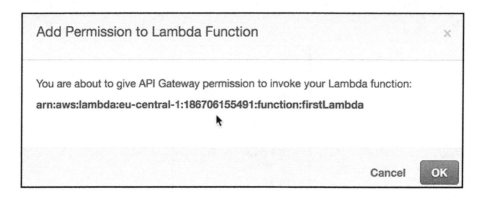

So remember from the beginning that you need to give your API permission to invoke your Lambda function; otherwise, just anyone can invoke your Lambda function, which you don't want. Click on **OK**.

Now, we have created an integration between our API and our Lambda function. Let's click on the little **Test** button, as shown in the following screenshot:

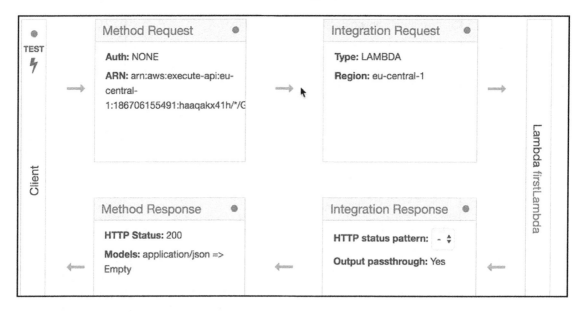

Once you click it, you will be able to execute an HTTP GET request by scrolling down the page and clicking on the **TEST** button.

Within 90 milliseconds, we will get a response back—**Hello from Lambda**, as seen in the following screenshot:

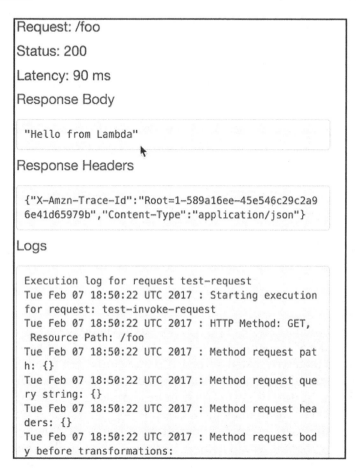

So it looks like we really invoked our Lambda function, but can we be sure? Let's check. Go back, and click on the foo resource and then click on the GET method. Now we can see our integration again, and on the right-hand side, you can see the Lambda function that I have integrated my API with. Click on it and you will be directed to the Lambda dashboard with your Lambda function. Let's take a look at the **Monitoring** tab:

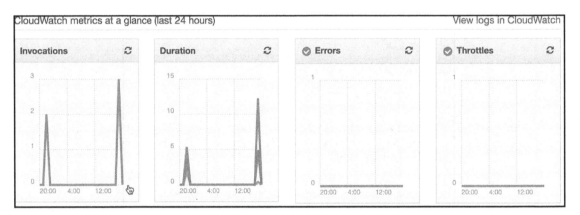

As you can see, it has in fact just been invoked—a couple of times, actually.

Summary

In this chapter, we learned a couple of things: how to navigate the AWS web dashboard, and how to navigate the Management Console. We also created and tested our first Lambda function and then we created a REST API and connected it to Lambda. Then we invoked the API, and through the API, we invoked our Lambda function. As you can imagine, it can become quite tedious to create more complex applications if we do it all on the Management Console. The Management Console is great for getting started, but it's not the right tool for building serious applications. It would be great if there was a programmatic framework that would help us to do that. Thankfully, there is. In the next chapter, we will explore the Serverless framework, which is a development framework that helps you to build serverless applications. See you there.

2
Exploring the Serverless Framework

In the previous chapter, we learned how to use the AWS Management Console to create Lambda functions and APIs. Now, we will use the Serverless framework to programmatically create APIs and Lambda functions. We will use the serverless command-line interface to deploy and test our functions. This will tremendously speed up our development processes.

The term **serverless** generally refers to applications that make heavy use of third-party cloud services, such as AWS Lambda. These services are also sometimes referred to as cloud functions, serverless microservices, or serverless functions. This doesn't mean that there are no servers involved anymore, just that you haven't installed to manage and operate these servers yourself. This is handled by the cloud provider, who takes care of things like scalability, high availability, security, performance, and so on. Here, we will be able to take a deeper look at using the Serverless framework to programmatically deploy and test Lambda functions, using the serverless command-line interface via local function invocation and remote function invocation.

In this chapter, we are going to cover the following topics:

- The Serverless framework
- Creating a serverless project
- Programming a lambda function with Node.js
- Testing and debugging lambda functions

The Serverless framework

Here, we are going to take a look at the Serverless framework documentation. We will then take a look at how to install it, and then we'll try out our first commands.

Go to the main landing page of the Serverless framework, serverless.com.

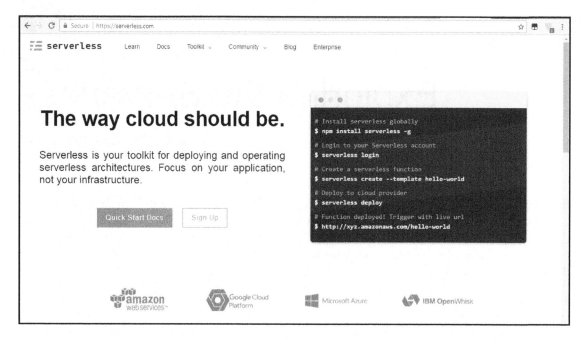

To find all the information that you need, click on **Quick Start Docs**. For now, let's take a quick look at the installation section. The first thing that you need to have installed is Node.js, and you will find some information on how to install it on your local machine. For programming **serverless**, we need Node.js version 4 or higher. If you don't have Node.js already, please do so now, and then resume.

Serverless runs on Node 4 or higher. For installing, go to the official Node.js website, download, and follow the installation instructions. If you want to see if Node has been installed successfully, just run node --version in Terminal. You will be able to see the corresponding Node version number printed out.

Once you open Terminal, the first thing that you need to check is if you have the right version of Node installed. Here, I am using Node version 6, which is higher than 4:

```
node --version
```

Next, I'll type in a command using **npm (node package manager)** to install the Serverless framework. It is better to install it globally so that it can be accessed anywhere by Terminal, no matter which directory it is in. This will download all the required dependencies and set up a path so that it can execute the serverless commands for the command line:

```
npm install -g serverless
```

Here, I have installed the newest version of serverless which, at the time of writing, is version 1.6.1:

```
+-- update-notifier@2.5.0
+-- boxen@1.3.0
| +-- ansi-align@2.0.0
| | `-- string-width@2.1.1
| |   +-- is-fullwidth-code-point@2.0.0
| |   `-- strip-ansi@4.0.0
| |     `-- ansi-regex@3.0.0
| +-- camelcase@4.1.0
| +-- cli-boxes@1.0.0
| +-- string-width@2.1.1
| | +-- is-fullwidth-code-point@2.0.0
| | `-- strip-ansi@4.0.0
| |   `-- ansi-regex@3.0.0
| +-- term-size@1.2.0
| | `-- execa@0.7.0
| |   +-- cross-spawn@5.1.0
| |   | +-- lru-cache@4.1.3
| |   | | +-- pseudomap@1.0.2
| |   | | `-- yallist@2.1.2
| |   | +-- shebang-command@1.2.0
| |   | | `-- shebang-regex@1.0.0
| |   | `-- which@1.3.1
| |   |   `-- isexe@2.0.0
| |   +-- npm-run-path@2.0.2
| |   | `-- path-key@2.0.1
| |   +-- p-finally@1.0.0
| |   `-- strip-eof@1.0.0
| `-- widest-line@2.0.0
|   `-- string-width@2.1.1
|     +-- is-fullwidth-code-point@2.0.0
|     `-- strip-ansi@4.0.0
|       `-- ansi-regex@3.0.0
+-- configstore@3.1.2
| +-- dot-prop@4.2.0
| | `-- is-obj@1.0.1
| `-- unique-string@1.0.0
|   `-- crypto-random-string@1.0.0
+-- import-lazy@2.1.0
+-- is-ci@1.1.0
+-- is-installed-globally@0.1.0
| +-- global-dirs@0.1.1
| `-- is-path-inside@1.0.1
|   `-- path-is-inside@1.0.2
+-- is-npm@1.0.0
+-- latest-version@3.1.0
| `-- package-json@4.0.1
|   +-- registry-auth-token@3.3.2
|   `-- registry-url@3.1.0
+-- semver-diff@2.1.0
| `-- xdg-basedir@3.0.0
+-- uuid@2.0.3
+-- write-file-atomic@2.3.0
| +-- imurmurhash@0.1.4
| `-- signal-exit@3.0.2
`-- yaml-ast-parser@0.0.34
```

Now, I can type in the serverless command, as shown in the following screenshot:

The previous screenshot shows all the sub-commands that can be used for the serverless command-line interface. If you haven't completed the installation and setup steps from Chapter 1, *Getting Started with AWS*, you need to execute the `config credentials` command, as given above. The Serverless framework needs to access your AWS account to execute certain AWS commands on your behalf. It needs to be able to create resources, modify resources, and delete resources. Instead of typing `serverless`, you can also use the `sls` shortcut:

Now that we have installed the Serverless framework, let's create our first serverless project.

Creating a serverless project

In the previous section, we installed the Serverless framework and tried out the command line. Now, let's create our first serverless project. We are going to use the Serverless framework to create a simple Node.js lambda function and a REST API. Open Terminal and create a directory where you can place your serverless project files. I named it `app`, but you can name it whatever you want. Go to that directory and open your preferred IDE. I used the Atom editor. When the Atom editor was opened in my empty directory, I used an Atom package at terminal plus to open a new Terminal window inside my IDE. This makes it easier because I don't need to switch between writing code and typing in commands. So, let's type in a command to scaffold a serverless service:

```
serverless create --template aws-nodejs
```

The command for creating a service is created, but it needs two more parameters. The first parameter is a `template`, and here we specify the cloud provider, in our case AWS, and the runtime, Node.js.

This command is a bit lengthy, so let's use a shorter command.

Instead of typing `template`, you can type `-t`. And, instead of typing `serverless`, we can type `sls`. Now, we need one more parameter, the name of our service. I call it `simple`, the simple service. But, we can also make this shorter, `-n`:

```
sls create -t aws-nodejs -n simple
```

Let's execute this command to create some boilerplate code. And there we go. Two files have been created, the `severless.yml` file which describes our project, and a `handler.js` implementation of my Lambda function handler:

```
C:\Users\admin\Desktop\programming-aws-lambda-master\javascript\blog-app>sls create -t aws-nodejs -n blog
Serverless: Generating boilerplate...

              The Serverless Application Framework
                   serverless.com, v1.27.3

Serverless: Successfully generated boilerplate for template: "aws-nodejs"
```

Let's take a look at the `serverless.yml` file first:

```
service: simple
```

Here, you find the configuration for our service, the name of our service that I've typed into the command line, the provider AWS, and our runtime Node.js. There are also some other configurations.

```
provider:
    name: aws
    runtime: nodejs4.3
```

Most of them can stay in the defaults, but the region is not right. I want another region. So, the default region is in `us-east, North Virginia`, and I want to use Frankfurt, so let's change that. Let's change it from `us-east-1` to `eu-central-1`:

```
provider:
    name: aws
    runtime: nodejs4.3
    stage: dev
    region: eu-central-1
```

There are some more configurations down here, such as IAM permissions, and we'll go into detail on that later. Scroll down a bit further and you will find our Lambda function, as shown next:

```
functions:
    hello:
        handler: handler.hello
```

The function name is `hello`, and the function `handler` is specified as well.

It references a file, our `handler.js` file that we created earlier, and that file exports a `hello` module. Let's take a look at the `handler.js` file:

```
'use strict';

module.exports.hello = Kevent, context, callback) => {
  const response = {
    statusCode: 200,
    body: JSON.stringify({
      message: 'Go Serverless v1.0! Your function executed success
      input: event,
    }),
  };
```

```
callback(null, response);

// Use this code if you don't use the http event with the LAMBDA-

integration
// callback(null, { message: 'Go Serverless v1.0! Your function
executed successfully', event });
};
```

You will see that it exports a function, our handler named `hello`. And, the signature looks familiar to what we have seen before. We have an event parameter, context parameter, and an optional callback parameter. The boilerplate code specifies a response that says `Go Serverless` and plays back the event that has been received. Then, it invokes a callback, an error-first callback, without an error, where we can specify the response.

Now, you can deploy this function using `sls deploy`. We need to give it the function name hello, for `-f`:

sls deploy -f hello

Now, this takes a little time. What happens behind the scenes is that serverless sets up some cloud formation templates, uploads them into an S3 bucket in our AWS S3 account, and uses these templates to create other AWS resources, such as our Lambda function. Now, our Lambda function has been deployed into the `eu-central-1` region using the `dev` stage:

```
Service Information
service: blog
stage: dev
region: eu-central-1
stack: blog-dev
api keys:
  None
endpoints:
  POST - https://58pletzc5d.execute-api.eu-central-1.amazonaws.com/dev/articles
  GET - https://58pletzc5d.execute-api.eu-central-1.amazonaws.com/dev/articles/{id}
  PUT - https://58pletzc5d.execute-api.eu-central-1.amazonaws.com/dev/articles
  DELETE - https://58pletzc5d.execute-api.eu-central-1.amazonaws.com/dev/articles
  GET - https://58pletzc5d.execute-api.eu-central-1.amazonaws.com/dev/articles
functions:
  hello: blog-dev-hello
  createArticle: blog-dev-createArticle
  readOneArticle: blog-dev-readOneArticle
  updateArticle: blog-dev-updateArticle
  deleteArticle: blog-dev-deleteArticle
  readAllArticles: blog-dev-readAllArticles
```

We haven't deployed any endpoints yet. And, the function name is `simple`, the name of our service; `dev` is the name of our stage; and `hello` is the name of our function. We can invoke the remote function from our command line by using `sls invoke` and giving it the function name `hello`. And, as you can see, we get back the message that we have specified in the `handler.js` boilerplate code:

```
sls invoke -f hello
{
        "statusCode": 200,
        "body": "{\"message\":"Go Sreverless v1.0! Your function executed
        successfully!\",\"input\":{}}"
}
```

If you want to do a lot of testing, it would take too much time to always deploy the function and then invoke the function via `sls invoke`, so you can also locally invoke the function. Simply add the parameter `sls invoke local`:

```
sls invoke local -f hello
```

This will call our function locally. Let's take an example. Let's change our function in the current boilerplate code to `Hello World!` as shown in the following screenshot:

```
'use strict';
module.exports.hello = (event, context, callback) => {
    const response = {
        statusCode: 200,
        body: JSON.stringify({
            message: 'Hello World!',
            input: event,
        }),
```

I've only changed my code locally. I didn't deploy it, so if I invoke it locally again, it shows `Hello World!` as shown here:

```
sls invoke local -f hello
{
        "statusCode" 200,
        "body": "{\"message\":\"Hello World!\",\"input\":\"\"}'
}
```

If the remote function is invoked, it shows `Go Serverless`:

```
sls invoke -f hello
{
        "statusCode": 200,
```

```
    "body": "{\"message\":"Go Sreverless v1.0! Your function executed
    successfully!\",\"input\":{}}"
}
```

Now, what we need to do is to create an API. Let's go back to the serverless.yml file and scroll down a little bit further to our function. Here, we can already see a template; what we need to do is to create an API. Delete the comment code and comment out the events property, the http property, the path, and the method. What this will do is it will create a simple REST API for us, specifying a get method on this resource path. Let's choose a different resource path. Let's call it hello, as follows:

```
functions:
  hello:
    handler: handler.hello
    events:
      - http:
          path: hello
          method: get
          cors: true
```

Now, let's run sls deploy again, and once sls deploy has been executed, we will have an endpoint for our API:

```
Service Information
service: simple
stage: dev
region: eu-central-1
stack: simple-dev
api keys:
  None
endpoints:
  GET - https://iqknh40tnh.execute-api.eu-central-1.amazonaws.com/dev/hello
  POST - https://iqknh40tnh.execute-api.eu-central-1.amazonaws.com/dev/articles
  GET - https://iqknh40tnh.execute-api.eu-central-1.amazonaws.com/dev/articles/{id}
  PUT - https://iqknh40tnh.execute-api.eu-central-1.amazonaws.com/dev/articles
  DELETE - https://iqknh40tnh.execute-api.eu-central-1.amazonaws.com/dev/articles
  GET - https://iqknh40tnh.execute-api.eu-central-1.amazonaws.com/dev/articles
functions:
  hello: simple-dev-hello
```

Try it out in the browser. Copy and paste the URL and it will respond back with our message, **Hello World!**, and also with the event that it received from us, as shown here:

{"message":"hello world","input":{"resource":"/hello","path":"/hello","httpMethod":"GET","headers":{"Accept":"text/html,application/xhtml+xml,application/xml;q=0.9,image/webp,image/apng,*/*;q=0.8","Accept-Encoding":"gzip, deflate, br","Accept-Language":"en-US,en;q=0.9","CloudFront-Forwarded-Proto":"https","CloudFront-Is-Desktop-Viewer":"true","CloudFront-Is-Mobile-Viewer":"false","CloudFront-Is-SmartTV-Viewer":"false","CloudFront-Is-Tablet-Viewer":"false","CloudFront-Viewer-Country":"IN","Host":"iqknh4otn.execute-api.eu-central-1.amazonaws.com","upgrade-insecure-requests":"1","User-Agent":"Mozilla/5.0 (Windows NT 10.0; Win64; x64) AppleWebKit/537.36 (KHTML, like Gecko) Chrome/67.0.3396.79 Safari/537.36","Via":"2.0 7b637ad78077549638b500611f792222.cloudfront.net (CloudFront)","X-Amz-Cf-Id":"aDkMQjThO4VUxmbQpg7Hfyaw62R8Bob6_XAvEQNdHp2223xuNg_z12==","X-Amzn-Trace-Id":"Root=1-5b1a5b9c-6fc204daf8dfd42ezf6abb61a","X-Forwarded-For":"182.76.16.118, 54.182.242.125","X-Forwarded-Port":"443","X-Forwarded-Proto":"https"},"queryStringParameters":null,"pathParameters":null,"stageVariables":null,"requestContext":{"resourceId":"1vtb4f","resourcePath":"/hello","httpMethod":"GET","extendedRequestId":"IvJuyE8cFiAFhKg=","requestTime":"11/Jun/2018:11:00:46 +0000","path":"/dev/hello","accountId":"019859648260","protocol":"HTTP/1.1","stage":"dev","requestTimeEpoch":1518214b4d676,"requestId":"3i7eae27-8d66-11e8-bfd6-7b4388754d87","identity":{"cognitoIdentityPoolId":null,"accountId":null,"cognitoIdentityId":null,"caller":null,"sourceIp":"182.76.16.118","accessKey":null,"cognitoAuthenticationType":null,"cognitoAuthenticationProvider":null,"userArn":null,"userAgent":"Mozilla/5.0 (Windows NT 10.0; Win64; x64) AppleWebKit/537.36 (KHTML, like Gecko) Chrome/67.0.3396.79 Safari/537.36","user":null},"apiId":"iqknh4otn"},"body":null,"isBase64Encoded":false}}

Programming a Lambda function with Node.js

Now, let's learn a little bit more about programming Lambda functions with Node.js. We are going to take a closer look at the function handler, and in particular its arguments, that is:

- Event objects
- Context objects
- Callback objects

Open the `handler.js` file and delete the code that's in the function body. One way to learn about the event and context object would be to log them out on the console:

```
'use strict';
module.exports.hello = (event, context, callback) => {
    console.log('event is', event);
};
```

Let's see what this gives us.

I am invoking the function locally to see what the output is with the function name set as `hello`:

```
sls invoke local -f hello
event is
```

Ok, my event, apparently, is null. Let's see what the context is, as shown next:

```
module.exports.hello = (event, context, callback) => {
    console.log('event is', event);
    console.log('context is', context);
};
```

The context actually gives me an object. Since we are invoking it locally, some information from this emulated or mocked local environment, for example, a hard coded string that says `id` for the AWS request ID, memory limits in megabytes, and so on, is shown here:

```
C:\Users\admin\Desktop\programming-aws-lambda-master\javascript\blog-app>sls invoke local -f hello
event is
context is { awsRequestId: 'id',
  invokeid: 'id',
  logGroupName: '/aws/lambda/simple-dev-hello',
  logStreamName: '2015/09/22/[HEAD]13370a84ca4ed8b77c427af260',
  functionVersion: 'HEAD',
  isDefaultFunctionVersion: true,
  functionName: 'simple-dev-hello',
  memoryLimitInMB: '1024',
  succeed: [Function: succeed],
  fail: [Function: fail],
  done: [Function: done],
  getRemainingTimeInMillis: [Function: getRemainingTimeInMillis] }
```

Let's change the code a little bit, and, instead of logging it out on the console, let's send it back via our callback as it was before. But this time, we not only give back the event but also some information from our context, such as the remaining time in milliseconds, the function name, and the request ID:

```
let remainingTime = context.getRemainingTimeInMillis();
let functionName = context.functionName;
let AWSrequestID = context.awsRequestId;

const response = {
    statusCode: 200,
    ev: event,
    rt: remainingTime,
    fn: functionName,
    aid: AWSrequestID
}
callback( null, response)
};
```

Let's invoke it locally first:

```
sls invoke local -f hello
```

```
{
    "statusCode": 200,
    "ev": "",
    "rt": 6000,
    "fn": "simple-dev-hello",
    "aid": "id"
}
```

Now, as shown in the previous screenshot, we get back the status code, the event doesn't exist, response time is a hard coded value of 6,000 milliseconds, the function name, and the hard coded ID.

Now, let's deploy our function and invoke it remotely:

```
sls deploy
```

Alright. Our function has been deployed:

```
region: eu-central-1
stack: simple-dev
api keys:
  None
endpoints:
  GET - https://nb2gqgav6i.execute-api.eu-central-1.amazonaws.com/dev/hello
  POST - https://nb2gqgav6i.execute-api.eu-central-1.amazonaws.com/dev/articles
  GET - https://nb2gqgav6i.execute-api.eu-central-1.amazonaws.com/dev/articles/{id}
  PUT - https://nb2gqgav6i.execute-api.eu-central-1.amazonaws.com/dev/articles
  DELETE - https://nb2gqgav6i.execute-api.eu-central-1.amazonaws.com/dev/articles
  GET - https://nb2gqgav6i.execute-api.eu-central-1.amazonaws.com/dev/articles
functions:
  hello: simple-dev-hello
  createArticle: simple-dev-createArticle
  readOneArticle: simple-dev-readOneArticle
  updateArticle: simple-dev-updateArticle
  deleteArticle: simple-dev-deleteArticle
  readAllArticles: simple-dev-readAllArticles
```

Once you invoke it remotely, you will observe the following:

```
{
    "statusCode": 200,
    "ev": {},
    "rt": 5998,
    "fn": "simple-dev-hello",
    "aid": "ca5f1156-ef0d-11e6-bdf4-df482d5dd82e"
}
```

Here, we can see that the remaining time in our remote execution is 5,998 milliseconds. The time, however, is specified by the default of six seconds, so at the point when the remaining time was calculated, we had used two milliseconds. Additionally, the ID of our request now also looks quite different from our local execution.

However, the event is still empty. Let's change that. Let's invoke our function with a synthetic event.

Create an `event.json` file and put a JSON object that says `foo` and `bar`, as follows:

```
{
    "foo": "bar"
}
```

Once that is done, go to the `handler.js` file and invoke the local function with the path to the `event.json` file. Instead of typing `path`, you can type `-p`, as follows:

```
sls invoke local -f hello -p event.json
```

And now, we get back the event that we have invoked the Lambda function with:

```
{
    "statusCode": 200,
    "ev": {
        "foo": "bar"
    },
    "rt": 6000,
    "fn": "simple-dev-hello",
    "aid": "id"
}
```

And, if invoked remotely, you will get the same event because it invokes the remote function with the local event in the `event.json` file.

OK. Let's take a quick look at the callback object. What happens if we don't provide a callback object? Can we still execute our Lambda function? Let's try it out. Let's invoke the local Lambda function. It doesn't throw an error, but it also doesn't give us a response either. What happens if we invoke the callback function without any arguments? It's basically the same as having no callback function at all. What about invoking it with null? This has the same effect. Now, how can we throw an error? We have an error-first callback function, so this should give us an error.

Testing and debugging Lambda functions

In the previous section, we learned about programming Lambda function handlers. Now, let's explore testing and debugging.

Here, we are going to look at three different testing and debugging approaches:

- Using the Serverless framework
- Using Postman for testing our API
- Using the AWS Management Console

Let's go back to our `handler.js` file from the previous section. There are a couple things that should be changed. The response method should be changed back to something that our API can work with.

Give it a `body` property with a `stringify` JSON content, as shown here:

```
body: JSON.stringify({
```

And, in the JSON content, get back the event in the remaining time from the context, and then, instead of returning an error, we will return the response:

```
'use strict';
module.exports.hello = (event, context, callback) => {
    let remainingTime = context.getRemainingTimeInMillis();
    let functionName = context.functionName;
    let AWSrequestID = context.awsRequestId;
    const response = {
        statusCode: 200,
        body: JSON.stringify({
            ev: event,
            rt: remainingTime
        })
    };
    callback(null, response);
};
```

After that, invoke the function locally by using the synthetic event:

```
sls invoke local -f hello -p event.json
{
    "statusCode": 200,
    "body": "{\"ev\":{\"foo\":\"bar\"},\"rt\":5000}"
}
```

Now, let's add some console log statements to the beginning of the function, and then log out the event and the context:

```
'use strict';
module.exports.hello = (event, context, callback) => {
    console.log('event is', event);
    console.log('context is', context);
    let remainingTime = context.getRemainingTimeInMillis();
    let functionName = context.functionName;
    let AWSrequestID = context.awsRequestId;
```

Once done, invoke the function:

```
C:\Users\admin\Desktop\programming-aws-lambda-master\javascript\blog-app> sls invoke local -f hello -p event.json
event is { foo: 'bar' }
context is { awsRequestId: 'id',
  invokeid: 'id',
  logGroupName: '/aws/lambda/simple-dev-hello',
  logStreamName: '2015/09/22/[HEAD]13370a84ca4ed8b77c427af260',
  functionVersion: 'HEAD',
  isDefaultFunctionVersion: true,
  functionName: 'simple-dev-hello',
  memoryLimitInMB: '1024',
  succeed: [Function: succeed],
  fail: [Function: fail],
  done: [Function: done],
  getRemainingTimeInMillis: [Function: getRemainingTimeInMillis] }
{
    "statusCode": 200,
    "body": "{\"ev\":{\"foo\":\"bar\"},\"rt\":6000}"
}
```

You should notice that the function has been invoked locally, and the console output is seen right before the response from the callback. Deploy the function and, once deployed, call the `invoke` command without the `local` sub-command:

```
sls invoke -f hello -p event.json
```

This will get the response from the callback. However, you won't be able to see the console log. So, how do we retrieve the remote logs?

Scroll over to the `sls` command; you will notice a `logs` sub-command:

```
config ...................... Configure Serverless
config credentials ........... Configures a new provider profile for the Serverless Framework
create ...................... Create new Serverless service
deploy ...................... Deploy a Serverless service
deploy function ............. Deploy a single function from the service
deploy list ................. List deployed version of your Serverless Service
deploy list functions ........ List all the deployed functions and their versions
info ........................ Display information about the service
install ..................... Install a Serverless service from GitHub or a plugin from the Serverless registry
invoke ...................... Invoke a deployed function
invoke local ................ Invoke function locally
logs ........................ Output the logs of a deployed function
metrics ..................... Show metrics for a specific function
```

Try using the `logs` sub-command with the function name `hello` as a parameter:

```
sls logs -f hello
```

You will be able to see the logs that have been retrieved from the AWS account, as shown here:

```
:\Users\admin\Desktop\programming-aws-lambda-master\javascript\blog-app>sls logs -f hello
START RequestId: 2e2f66f0-6e1f-11e8-bc0f-2dedd2183214 Version: $LATEST
2018-06-12 14:31:23.540 (+05:30)      2e2f66f0-6e1f-11e8-bc0f-2dedd2183214      event is { foo: 'bar' }
2018-06-12 14:31:23.607 (+05:30)      2e2f66f0-6e1f-11e8-bc0f-2dedd2183214      context is { callbackWaitsForEmptyEventLoop: [Getter/Setter],
  done: [Function],
  succeed: [Function],
  fail: [Function],
  logGroupName: '/aws/lambda/simple-dev-hello',
  logStreamName: '2018/06/12/[$LATEST]3e6ab0888f1d4af9b310ff2b986e80d0',
  functionName: 'simple-dev-hello',
```

This uses a service called CloudWatch. You can also see the `console-log` output event, and the context as well:

```
  memoryLimitInMB: '1024',
  functionVersion: '$LATEST',
  getRemainingTimeInMillis: [Function],
  invokeid: '2e2f66f0-6e1f-11e8-bc0f-2dedd2183214',
  awsRequestId: '2e2f66f0-6e1f-11e8-bc0f-2dedd2183214',
  invokedFunctionArn: 'arn:aws:lambda:eu-central-1:019859648260:function:simple-dev-hello' }
END RequestId: 2e2f66f0-6e1f-11e8-bc0f-2dedd2183214
REPORT RequestId: 2e2f66f0-6e1f-11e8-bc0f-2dedd2183214  Duration: 70.29 ms      Billed Duration: 100 ms      Memory Size: 1024 MB      Max Memory Used: 27 MB
```

Also, as shown above, Amazon gives some additional information, such as the duration used. So, in the preceding screenshot, we actually just used 60 milliseconds, but because it's rounded up to the nears 100, we are billed for 100 milliseconds. We have configured our Lambda function with 1 GB of memory, but we only used 9 MB. Such information is also useful for cost-optimization purposes.

Testing the API using Postman

Now, we are going to use Postman to test the API. If you don't have Postman installed on your computer yet, you can get it at `getpostman.com` and install it on your local operating system.

So, let's test the API. Open Postman and enter the URL that is to serve as the endpoint for our service. To retrieve the URL, head back to Terminal. You can get the information about our service by typing `sls info`, which will provide several pieces of information including the required endpoint that is the URL. Copy the endpoint and enter the URL. Select the appropriate HTTP method – in our case, it's the `get` method—and send the request:

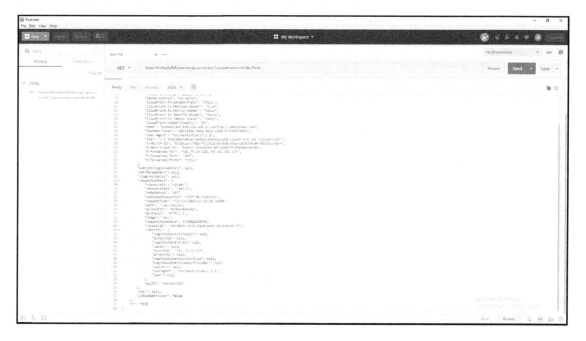

As shown previously, we get back the response, including the required event.

Testing and debugging via the AWS Management Console

Sign in to our Management Console and go to the API Gateway Service. We will see our new API that we created with a Serverless framework. Since we have done this before, I will briefly recap the process. Click on the **hello** part and `get` method, and click on the Test icon to get the following screenshot:

Scroll down and click on **Test**, which will give you the same information as given previously in Postman.

Go back to our resource path and `get` method, and head over to the Lambda function, which can be found on the right-hand side, as shown here:

Once you get into the Lambda function, click on the **Monitoring** tab to view the logs on the AWS Management Console dashboard. You will see some CloudWatch metrics with various invocations and durations, as shown here:

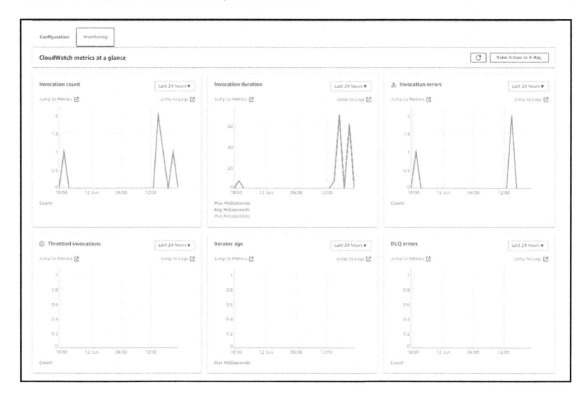

You can access the logs by clicking on **View logs in CloudWatch**, which will show a number of logs that appeared over time for the Lambda function, as shown as follows:

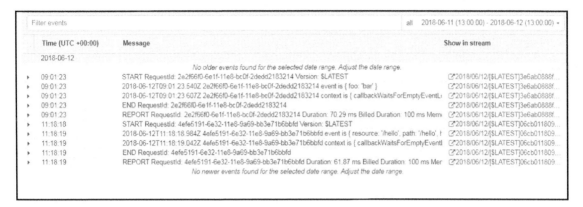

It takes a little bit of time for these logs to materialize, so if you invoke a remote Lambda function and instantly (or after just a fraction of a second) you try to retrieve the logs, you won't be successful. If you click on these logs, you can see the event and context logs, which is the information that is retrieved with the first approach using the Serverless framework. Using the Serverless framework, it's much easier and much more convenient to retrieve these logs than clicking through your AWS Management Console.

Summary

In this chapter, we learned how to use the Serverless framework to create and test Lambda functions and APIs, and we tried out different approaches for API testing, Lambda testing, and debugging. Now, we have all the things necessary to build a real application, so in the next chapter, that's what we are going to do, by building a serverless application.

3
Building a Serverless Application

In this chapter, we are going to build a web application using a combination of different technologies. For that, we will again be using the serverless framework with Lambda and API Gateway, but we will also use a couple of other AWS services, particularly DynamoDB to preserve our data. We will also be using Cognito to identify users, and then we will use S3 and CloudFront to deploy our front app.

In this chapter, we are going to cover the following topics:

- Building a stateless, serverless web application backend
- Creating a stateful, serverless backend with DynamoDB
- Creating a web client
- Deploying a serverless frontend on CloudFront

Let's dive in!

Building a stateless serverless web application backend

Here, we are going to build the stateless web application backend, and later on we will add the database. This application will allow users to create, read, update, and delete blog articles. Then we will deploy and test our little blog API.

Open the Atom text editor in the empty `blog-app` directory. Let's use the command line to create some files:

```
sls create -t aws-nodejs -n blog
```

I have used `sls` create to create a new service, but with a new name—`blog`.

This command line will generate two files, `serverless.yml` and `handler.js`, as shown in the following screenshot:

Open the `serverless.yml` file and delete some of the comments. Once that is done, the next thing you must do is change the region. Here, I am deploying my service in the Frankfurt region in `eu-central-1`, as follows:

```
service: blog
provider:
  name: aws
  runtime: nodejs4.3
  stage: dev
  region: eu-central-1
```

Now, scroll down to the function. You have to change the name of the Lambda function from hello to something like `createArticle`. Once that is done, we need to rename the module that gets exported to the `handler.js` file, as follows:

```
functions:
  createArticle:
    handler: handler.createArticle
```

Since the module that the Lambda function references as a `handler` function has been renamed, you also need to rename it in the `handler.js` file. So replace `hello` with `createArticle`, as shown in the following screenshot:

```
'use strict';
module.exports.createArticle = (event, context, callback) =>
  const response = {
    statusCode: 200,
    body: JSON.stringify({
```

```
        message: 'Go Serverless v1.0! Your function executed
successfully!',
        input: event,
    }),
  };
```

Once that is done, let's go back to the `serverless.yml` file and add our API Gateway:

```
functions:
  createArticle:
    handler: handler.createArticle
    events:
      - http:
          path: users/create
          method: get
```

So the things that must be changed are the path and the method. For consistency, let's name the path `createArticle`, while the method should be named the `post` method rather than the `get` method:

```
functions:
  createArticle:
    handler: handler.createArticle
    events:
      - http:
          path: createArticle
          method: post
```

Now let's deploy our service by typing `sls deploy`:

```
sls deploy
```

The following screenshot shows the deployed service:

```
C:\Users\admin\Desktop\programming-aws-lambda-master\javascript\blog-app>sls deploy
Serverless: Packaging service...
Serverless: Excluding development dependencies...
Serverless: Creating Stack...
Serverless: Checking Stack create progress...
.....
Serverless: Stack create finished...
Serverless: Uploading CloudFormation file to S3...
Serverless: Uploading artifacts...
Serverless: Uploading service .zip file to S3 (5.96 KB)...
Serverless: Validating template...
Serverless: Updating Stack...
Serverless: Checking Stack update progress...
...............................................................................
Serverless: Stack update finished...
Service Information
service: blog
stage: dev
region: eu-central-1
stack: blog-dev
api keys:
  None
endpoints:
  POST - https://9owl38dug8.execute-api.eu-central-1.amazonaws.com/dev/articles
  GET - https://9owl38dug8.execute-api.eu-central-1.amazonaws.com/dev/articles
  PUT - https://9owl38dug8.execute-api.eu-central-1.amazonaws.com/dev/articles
  DELETE - https://9owl38dug8.execute-api.eu-central-1.amazonaws.com/dev/deleteArticle
functions:
  createArticle: blog-dev-createArticle
  readArticle: blog-dev-readArticle
  updateArticle: blog-dev-updateArticle
  deleteArticle: blog-dev-deleteArticle
```

Once it is deployed, invoke the Lambda function and see if it works:

```
C:\Users\admin\Desktop\programming-aws-lambda-master\javascript\blog-app>sls invoke -f createArticle
{
    "statusCode": 200,
    "body": "{\"ev\":{},\"rt\":5929}"
}
```

Next, let's use Postman to check whether the API also works. For that purpose, we will need the endpoint that is provided in the preceding code. Copy the link and open Postman.

In Postman, enter the request URL. Since a `post` method has been deployed, switch the tab to **Post** and click **Send**:

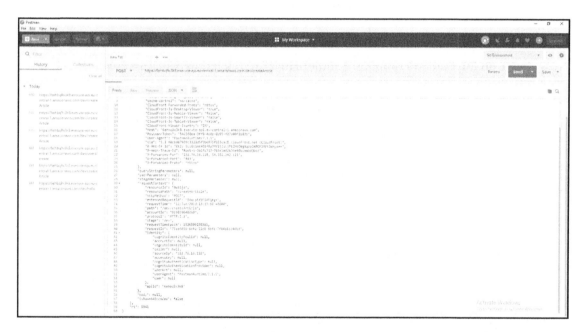

Now, you can change the file structure by going back to the editor and changing it.

Let's do that!

Changing the file structure

Go back to the `blog-app` directory. The first thing we need to do before restructuring the code is to create a `subdirectory` named `articles`, as shown in the following screenshot:

Now, move all the Lambda function handlers that are related to articles to the `articles` file. Once this is done, you will have the `createArticle` function in the `handler.js` file:

However, there are different ways in which you can structure your Lambda function handlers and determine how many Lambda functions you want to deploy per service. For instance, here I would like to have one Lambda function per method; let's rename the `handler.js` file to `create.js`, thereby reflecting what the Lambda function actually does. You also need to change the name of the handler from `createArticle` to `handler`:

```
module.exports.handler = (event, context, callback) => {
    const response = {
        statusCode: 200,
        body: JSON.stringify({
            message: 'Go Serverless v1.0! Your function executed
successfully!',
            input: event,
        }),
```

We should also update our `serverless.yml` file. Scroll down to the functions.

We need to change the function name and the function that should be exported. Since the path of the function handler has changed, it will be in the articles `subdirectory` under the filename `create`. The function that is exported is not `createArticle` anymore, but `handler`:

```
functions:
  createArticle:
    handler: articles/create.handler
    events:
      - http:
          path: createArticle
          method: post
#       - s3: ${env:BUCKET}
#       - schedule: rate(10 minutes)
```

So here, the Lambda function is named `createArticle` and the function handler is the article `subdirectory`. The file is named `create` and is a function `handler`, so why not name it handler?

Once that is done, let's remove the dummy code from the function handler and replace it with something else. The first thing that should be done is to parse the event object. Since it is an HTTP event, it should have a `body` property. I saved the `body` property in a constant named `data`:

```
'use strict'

module.exports.handler = {event, context, callback) => {
    const data = JSON.parse(event.body);
    if (typeof data.text !== 'string') {
        console.error('Validation Failed');
        callback(new Error('Body did not contain a text property.'));
        return;
    }
};
```

Now let's assume that it has a certain structure and that the `data` object has a text property of the `string` type. We also need to check that the code conforms to the following screenshot:

```
module.exports.handler = {event, context, callback} => {
    const data = JSON.parse(event.body);
    if (data.text && typeof data.text !== 'string') {
```

```
            console.error('Validation Failed');
            callback(new Error('Body did not contain a text property.'));
            return;
    }
};
```

If the validation fails, then the error must be logged on the console so that the callback message can be sent.

Next, for debugging purposes, log out of the text property on the console and prepare a response message for the callback that has a status code of 200, which will send back a message stating Created article, as shown in the following screenshot. Once done, invoke the callback with a response:

```
module.exports.handler = {event, context, callback} => {
    const data = JSON.parse(event.body);
    if (data.text && typeof data.text !== 'string') {
        console.error('Validation Failed');
        callback(new Error('Body did not contain a text property.'));
        return;
    }
    console.log(data.text);
    const respose = {
        statusCode: 200,
        body: JSON.stringify({
            message: 'Created article.'
        }),
    };
    callback(null, response);
};
```

Let's deploy our service and try it out:

```
endpoints:
  POST - https://9owl38dug8.execute-api.eu-central-1.amazonaws.com/dev/articles
  GET - https://9owl38dug8.execute-api.eu-central-1.amazonaws.com/dev/articles
  PUT - https://9owl38dug8.execute-api.eu-central-1.amazonaws.com/dev/articles
  DELETE - https://9owl38dug8.execute-api.eu-central-1.amazonaws.com/dev/deleteArticle
```

The service has been deployed. Now we will head back to Postman to test the API.

We will again send a `post` request, but this time we will click with a **Body** (found in the tab). It should be JSON-encoded and contain the text `hello world`, as shown in the following screenshot:

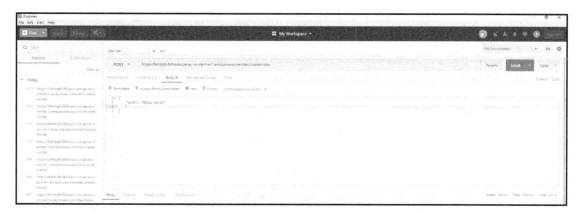

Now click on **Send**, et voila-it says **Created article**:

Let's now go back to Terminal and check the logs. To check the logs, type in `sls logs` and our function name, `createArticle`:

We can see in the logs that it says `hello world`, as shown in the following screenshot:

Creating more functions

Alright. Let's create some more functions.

First, I will create or specify the functions that I want to have. I'm going to create an API for reading articles, for updating articles, and for deleting articles, as shown in the following screenshot:

```
readArticle:
   handler: articles/read.handler
   events:
     - http:
         path: articles
         method: get
updateArticle:
   handler: articles/update.handler
   events:
     - http:
         path: articles
         method: put
deleteArticle:
   handler: articles/delete.handler
   events:
     - http:
         path: articles
         method: delete
```

You also need to create the files. Create three separate files under the articles files `serverless.js`, `read.js`, and `update.js`.

Now, let's go back to the `create.js` file, copy the code, and paste it into the `read.js` file. Once this is done, delete the following from the `read.js` file:

```
const data = JSON.parse(event.body);
if (data.text && typeof data.text !== 'string') {
    console.error('Validation Failed');
    callback(new Error('Body did not contain a text property.'));
    return;
}
```

For now, let's simply create a stub because you can't save data yet, and it doesn't really make sense to do anything else. Rename the message function with respect to the filename.

In the `read.js` file, enter the following:

```
'use strict'
module.exports.handler = (event, context, callback) => {
    const response = {
        statusCode: 200,
        body: JSON.stringify({
          message: 'Read article.'
        }),
    };
    callback(null, response);
};
```

In the `update.js` file, enter the following:

```
'use strict'
module.exports.handler = (event, context, callback) => {
    const response = {
        statusCode: 200,
        body: JSON.stringify({
          message: 'Update article.'
        }),
    };
    callback(null, response);
};
```

In the `delete.js` file, enter the following:

```
'use strict'
module.exports.handler = (event, context, callback) => {
    const response = {
        statusCode: 200,
        body: JSON.stringify({
          message: 'Delete article.'
        }),
    };
    callback(null, response);
};
```

We also need to save the `serverless.yml` file.

Alright. Let's deploy our service.

Once deployed, you will get four functions:

```
functions:
    createArticle: blog-dev-createArticle
    readArticle: blog-dev-readArticle
    updateArticle: blog-dev-updateArticle
    deleteArticle: blog-dev-deleteArticle
```

You will also get four endpoints:

```
endpoints:
  POST - https://9owl38dug8.execute-api.eu-central-1.amazonaws.com/dev/articles
  GET - https://9owl38dug8.execute-api.eu-central-1.amazonaws.com/dev/articles
  PUT - https://9owl38dug8.execute-api.eu-central-1.amazonaws.com/dev/articles
  DELETE - https://9owl38dug8.execute-api.eu-central-1.amazonaws.com/dev/deleteArticle
```

Make sure that you remove the `CreateArticle` path and also name its articles; otherwise, the Management Console will show that our API has a little inconsistency.

Now let's check the AWS Management Console:

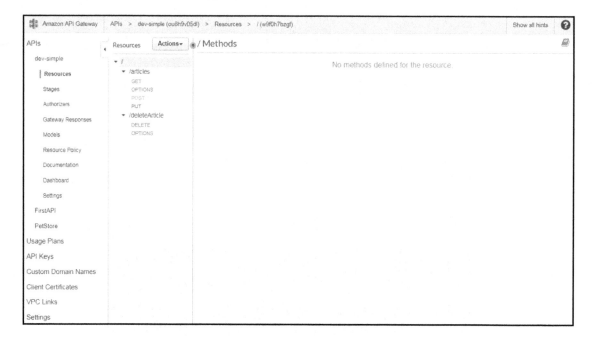

As shown in the screenshot, we have a DELETE, GET, POST, and PUT method. If you click on the method, it also shows the API integration with our Lambda function.

In the next section, we are going to add DynamoDB to our backend and make it a stateful, serverless application.

Creating a stateful serverless backend with DynamoDB

By now, you will know how to create a stateless web application. Now we are going to add a database to our backend. For this purpose, we will create a DynamoDB database table and then use the DynamoDB node.js client to create, read, update, and delete items. We will then add this functionality to our little blog application.

So let's get started.

Sign in to the AWS Management Console (the location I have chosen in our example is Frankfurt) and open the DynamoDB dashboard. Since we don't have a DynamoDB table yet, As a service offering DynamoDB is the database. Hence, we don't need to manage the database server on our own. You can use the web dashboard to create tables by clicking on the **Create Table** button and going through the wizard. However, before that, we will need to use the serverless framework to programmatically create the DynamoDB table for us, so click on **Cancel** for now.

Go to the editor and open the serverless.yml file. You will notice that there will be a section where you can specify the resources that will be provisioned by using CloudFormation. Replace the dummy code that was placed with the code that you prepare as follows:

```
    resources:
        Resources:
            BlogTable:
                Type: AWS::DynamoDB::Table
                Properties:
                    TableName: BlogTable
                    AttributeDefinitions:
                        - AttributeName: article_id
                          AttributeType: S
                    KeySchema:
                        - AttributeName: article_id
```

```
                    KeyType: HASH
            ProvisionedThroughput:
                ReadCapacityUnits: 1
                WriteCapacityUnits: 1
```

As shown in the preceding screenshot, I am creating a `BlogTable` resource for us. The `BlogTable` resource is of the `DynamoDB Table` type, and the `DynamoDB Table` type needs a couple of properties. For instance, it needs a `TableName`, which in this case is `BlogTable`. We have also specified the attributes—which of the attributes is the hash key and which one is the range key (range key can be optional). In this case, the hash key is `article_id`.

 The hash key in DynamoDB is something like a primary key or a partition key that you might know from other databases.

Another attribute that should be specified is `ProvisionedThroughput`, which can help in determining how much throughput is used, and can also determine the cost of the DynamoDB table.

 To learn more about the attributes, read the DynamoDB documentation.

Now open Terminal and go into the service directory. Simply type `sls` deploy to provision our DynamoDB table:

```
endpoints:
  POST - https://9owl38dug8.execute-api.eu-central-1.amazonaws.com/dev/articles
  GET - https://9owl38dug8.execute-api.eu-central-1.amazonaws.com/dev/articles
  PUT - https://9owl38dug8.execute-api.eu-central-1.amazonaws.com/dev/articles
  DELETE - https://9owl38dug8.execute-api.eu-central-1.amazonaws.com/dev/deleteArticle
functions:
  createArticle: blog-dev-createArticle
  readArticle: blog-dev-readArticle
  updateArticle: blog-dev-updateArticle
  deleteArticle: blog-dev-deleteArticle
```

As you can see from the preceding screenshot, the deployment has been finished, and we can now switch over to the AWS Management Console to see if the table has been created.

You will now see that a **BlogTable** is present, which is active and has a partition or hash key, which are synonyms for the name `article_id`.

For the next step, we need to connect our application to the DynamoDB table that we just created. For this purpose, we need to install a dependency, the *AWS SDK*.

Create a `package.json` file via `npm init -y`:

```
npm init -y
```

```
C:\Users\admin\Desktop\programming-aws-lambda-master\javascript\blog-app>npm init -y
Wrote to C:\Users\admin\Desktop\programming-aws-lambda-master\javascript\blog-app\package.json:

{
  "name": "blog-app",
  "version": "1.0.0",
  "description": "",
  "main": "handler.js",
  "scripts": {
    "test": "echo \"Error: no test specified\" && exit 1"
  },
  "keywords": [],
  "author": "",
  "license": "ISC"
}
```

Then install the dependency, via npm, with `i` for install and `-save` so it gets saved in the `package.json` file, `aws-sdk`.

Once the dependency has been installed, we will be able to see the `node_modules` directory with the `aws-sdk` and its dependencies . We will also see that the dependency has been added to our dependencies in the `package.json` file.

We will now go to the `create.js` file and connect our application to the DynamoDB table:

```
'use strict';
module.exports.handler = (event, context, callback) => {
  const data = JSON.parse(event.body);
    if (data.text && typeof data.text !== 'string'){
      console.error('Validation Failed');
      callback(new Error('Body did not contain a text property.'));
      return;
    }
  console.log(data.text);
  const response = {
  statusCode: 200,
  body: JSON.stringify({
  message: 'Created article.'
```

```
    }),
  }
callback(null, response);
};
```

You will notice that the create function handler just sends back some dummy data, a hard-coded response with an HTTP status code 200, and the JSON in the body. You might wonder about the structure of the response. There are different ways to integrate API Gateway with Lambda. This style is called Lambda proxy and it's the default that the serverless framework currently uses. Using this integration style, you can specify the HTTP and the HTTP request, programmatically. You could, for example, also add HTTP headers or other things programmatically. This is much more convenient than doing it on the AWS console, which you would need to do if you want to use the plain Lambda style instead of the Lambda proxy integration style.

The first thing that we need to do is add our dependencies to the create.js file. We need to add the aws-sdk, the module that I just installed. We then use AWS to create a new DynamoDB client. Since DynamoDB uses different clients, we will use the document client, which is a higher-level client that is easier to use, more convenient, and more developer friendly:

```
'use strict';

const AWS = require('aws-sdk');
const dynamo = new AWS.DynamoDB.DocumentClient();

module.exports.handler = (event, context, callback) => {
    const data = JSON.parse(event.body);
    if (data.text && typeof data.text !== 'string'){
        console.error('Validation Failed');
        callback(new Error('Body did not contain a text property.'));
        return;
    }
```

We then replace the console.log statement with a dynamo request, and issue a put request to create a new item:

```
dynamo.put(params, putCall)
const response = {
   statusCode: 200,
   body: JSON.stringify({
       message: 'Created article.'
   }),
};
```

The `put` method needs two arguments; the first of which is `params` and the second of which is `callback`. You also need to implement the `params` and the `callback`. You can look up the DynamoDB Node.js SDK documentation on how to do that.

First we need a JSON file that specifies the table name and specifies the item. For now, we will use a hard-coded ID, our `article_id`, and give the second attribute the text that is retrieved from our event. The second thing to do is specify `putCallback`. To do this, create a new variable, `callback`, and assign the method, which is an error-first callback function, as follows:

```
const params = {
    TableName: 'BlogTable',
    Item: {
        article_id "1",
        text: data.text
    },
};

const putCallback = (error, result) => {
if (error) {
    console.error(error);
    callback(new Error('Could not save record.'));
    return;
}
```

If there is an error, scroll down and copy the following:

```
const response = {
    statusCode: 200,
    body: JSON.stringify({
        message: 'Created article.'
    }),
};
callback(null, response);
```

Once you have copied the preceding code, prepare the response that should be sent back to the item that was created in DynamoDB. So, instead of sending back the object, we are going to send back the `result.Item`:

```
const putCallback = (error, result) => {
    if (error) {
        console.error(error);
        callback(new Error('Could not save record.'));
        return;
    }
    const response = {
```

```
                statusCode: 200,
                body: JSON.stringify(result.Item),

        };
        callback(null, response);
    }
    dynamo.put(params, putCallback);
```

 If you want to learn more about the structure of the result, you can log it out on the console and view it by entering the following:

```
console.log(result);
```

Now let's locally invoke our `createArticle` function with the `event.json` file, as shown in the following:

```
C:\Users\admin\Desktop\programming-aws-lambda-master\javascript\blog-app>sls invoke local -f createArticle -p articles/event.json
{
    "statusCode": 200
}
C:\Users\admin\Desktop\programming-aws-lambda-master\javascript\blog-app>
```

This returns the service code 200, and if we switch over to the AWS Management Console, we can see that the **Hello World** item has been created, as shown in the following screenshot:

However, if you want to create more articles, you would need to increase or change the `article_id` number. So what we need to do is add the following module:

```
npm i --save uuid
```

This will install the `uuid` module, which can be imported as shown in the following screenshot:

```
const AWS = require('aws-sdk');
const dynamo = new AWS.DynamoDB.DocumentClient();
const uuid = require('uuid');
```

Once done, you can replace your hard coded `article_id`:

```
const params = {
    TableName: 'BlogTable',
    Item: {
        article_id: uuid.v1(),
        text: data.text
    },
};
```

> The way the ID is used is by specifying the version number of the kind of `uuid` that you want to create.

Now switch back over to the management console and refresh the table. You will notice that an item has been created with a randomized `uuid`, as shown in the following screenshot:

Alright, it seems to work. But does it actually work if we deploy our service? Spoiler alert: it won't.

Nevertheless, we will deploy the service as it is currently and see what went wrong and what can be done to fix it if you run into the same error later.

Switch over to the editor and deploy the service via `sls deploy`:

```
sls deploy
```

Once the service has been deployed, invoke the command remotely. You will run into an error. Try getting more info on what went wrong. Check the logs as well. Scroll up the logs and you will notice the following:

We can see that our Lambda function is actually not authorized to perform the `PutItem` request on our `BlogTable` resource. So let's fix this. Go to our `serverless.yml` file. You will notice that you can add IAM statements or IAM roles to your service.

> By the way, this is supposed to change in serverless framework version 1.8. So if you're using a newer version of the serverless framework, please head over to the serverless website and check out the documentation.

If you are using serverless framework 1.7 or earlier, you can add the following IAM role statements, where you specify which kind of actions you want to perform:

```
provider:
  name: aws
  runtime: nodejs4.3
  stage: dev
  region: eu-centra-1
  iamRoleStatements:
  - Effect: Allow
    Action:
        - dynamodb: Query
        - dynamodb: GetItem
        - dynamodb: PutItem
        - dynamodb: UpdateItem
        - dynamodb: DeleteItem
    Resources: "PUT_YOUR_ARN_HERE"
```

From the preceding screenshot, you will notice that our resource ARN is missing. How do you find this?

Switch over to the AWS Management Console. On your DynamoDB table, there's a tab named Overview. Scroll down and you will be able to see the Amazon resource name. Copy the name and replace it with the missing ARN name in the `serverless.yml` file.

Once the service has been redeployed, invoke it:

```
C:\Users\admin\Desktop\programming-aws-lambda-master\javascript\blog-app>sls deploy
Serverless: Packaging service...
Serverless: Excluding development dependencies...
Serverless: Uploading CloudFormation file to S3...
Serverless: Uploading artifacts...
Serverless: Uploading service .zip file to S3 (6.48 MB)...
Serverless: Validating template...
Serverless: Updating Stack...
Serverless: Checking Stack update progress...
.................
Serverless: Stack update finished...
Service Information
service: blog
stage: dev
region: eu-central-1
stack: blog-dev
api keys:
  None
endpoints:
  POST - https://jdonclv412.execute-api.eu-central-1.amazonaws.com/dev/articles
  GET - https://jdonclv412.execute-api.eu-central-1.amazonaws.com/dev/articles
  PUT - https://jdonclv412.execute-api.eu-central-1.amazonaws.com/dev/articles
  DELETE - https://jdonclv412.execute-api.eu-central-1.amazonaws.com/dev/deleteArticle
functions:
  createArticle: blog-dev-createArticle
  readArticle: blog-dev-readArticle
  updateArticle: blog-dev-updateArticle
  deleteArticle: blog-dev-deleteArticle

C:\Users\admin\Desktop\programming-aws-lambda-master\javascript\blog-app>sls invoke -f createArticle -p articles/event.json
{
    "statusCode": 200
}
```

As you can see in the preceding code, we get back a status code of 200. When we check the table, we will be able to see that a third item has been added, as shown in the following screenshot:

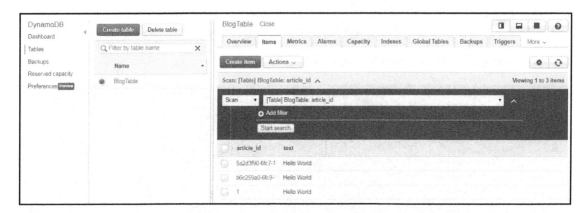

Before we move on to implementing the read, update, and delete functions, we need to refactor our code a little bit, because right now, the persistence business logic and Lambda function code is all tangled together and should be separated. If you want to use test-driven development, write unit tests, or something similar, separating the business logic from your Lambda function can come in quite handy.

So, let's create a `model.js` file:

```javascript
'use strict';
const uuid = require('uuid');
class Article {
    constructor{id, text) {
        this.article_id = id;
        this.text = text;
    }
}
const createArticle = (event, callback) => {
    validateAttributes(event, callback);
    const body = JSON.parse(event.body);
    const id = uuid.v1();
    const text = body.text;
    return new Article(id, text):
}
const readArticle = (event, callback) => {
    validateId(event, callback);
    const body = JSON.parse(event.body);
    const id = body.article_id;
    return new Article(id);
}
const updateArticle = (event, callback) => {
    validateId(event, callback);
    validateAttributes(event, callback);
    const body = JSON.parse(event.body);
    const id = body.article_id;
    const text = body.text;
    return new Article(id, text);
}
```

As you can see, I have created an `article` class that captures the properties of the article. Then there are some helper methods, such as `createArticle`, that transform the Lambda function event and callback, and use these in a validation step, which will then create an article object and return that article object using the event information. We also have some more helper functions for validating our event and throwing an error if the validation fails. Then we export our article class and the create, read, update, and delete methods.

One more layer of abstraction that I want to add is a data access object for DynamoDB.

I've already prepared something for that. I'm going to create a new `subdirectory`, `util`, and in that `subdirectory`, I will create a file named `dynamo-dao.js`. Again, we just copy and paste the source code. Don't worry, it's all in the repository; you can look it up there.

Basically, what we are going to do is wrap the DynamoDB document client in a class and provide some higher-level methods that take the model as an input, so my article and a callback, and so we pass in our callback into the Dynamo method, such as a put method, and if the put method works out correctly, we call our callback here.

We would pass in the callback from our Lambda function to create a new item. One more thing that should be created is a controller. You can judge for yourself whether you need so many levels of abstraction, or if fewer levels would do.

Let's create a new file, `controller.js`, and add our controller code here. What this does is it wraps around the DynamoDB data access object and wraps or performs the error handling so that we have it in the main code. We import the `createArticle` method from my `model.js` file and import DynamoDAO and the controller. The way we use them is to use the `createArticle` method here to create a model from our event. By using my callback, if there's an error, I can send the error to my callback function. Here, I am creating a DynamoDAO and passing in the Dynamo client from up here, as well as the name of my table, which is `BlogTable`. Then I'm creating a controller, my `ArticleController`, passing in my DynamoDAO. Last but not least, I invoke the `createArticle` method on my controller, giving it my model and my callback from up here. The delete method looks very similar—`deleteArticle`. Update just changes to `updateArticle`. Now, let's deploy our service.

Once deployed, invoke the service. Invoking the service will create a new article that can be seen when you switch to the AWS Management Console, and you will see an article with the name **Hello Universe**.

Let's now try to invoke the `readArticle` method. For that, you need to specify the `article_id`. Switch to the AWS Management Console, copy one of the article IDs, and paste it into the `event.json` file. Invoke the `readArticle` function and you will get back **Hello World**. Let's try updating. Instead of `Hello World`, let's replace it with `Hello Universe`, and instead of `readArticle`, let's use `updateArticle`. When you read it again, you will notice that it says **Hello Universe**. And last but not least, you can try the same in the delete article. Go back to the table and refresh. The article will be gone.

Creating a web client

In the previous section, we created a Cognito pool and added some functionality to our backend to retrieve the Cognito identity from our context object. Here, we will create a web frontend for our application, a web client. We will first generate a JavaScript SDK of our service using API Gateway, and then we will use this SDK with a Cognito client in a simple web page. Open the **Amazon Cognito** dashboard from the AWS Management Console. To use the Cognito site, go to **Services** and type in `Cognito`.

Cognito is a web service that allows you to manage or implement sign-up and sign-in functionality for your application. There are two options that are provided on the Cognito site: **Manage your User Pools and Manage Federated Identities**. You can create your own Cognito pool or you can use federated identities if you want to allow your users to authenticate, for example, using a Facebook or Google account. It also allows unauthenticated identities. Authorization and highly customized pools can be a bit out of the scope of this section. Instead, we will focus on how to use Cognito IDs to identify users within their Lambda functions.

So now, we will select the federated identities option in Cognito to create a Cognito pool. Click on the **Manage Federated Identities** button and give the **Identity pool** a name (in this example, I have used the name `BlogPool`). Setting up authentication providers can take a long time, so we will use unauthenticated identities by clicking on **Enable access to unauthenticated identities** and creating a new pool:

You will see from the preceding screenshot that what has been created for us is an IAM role that is connected to our Cognito pool, so you can specify what access rights or access permissions the users get that are identified via Cognito. You can then differentiate between the unauthenticated identities and authenticated identities, as shown in the preceding screenshot.

Click on **Allow** and you will see that the Cognito pool has been created and that Amazon has provided us with some sample data that we can use with source code on various platforms such as JavaScript, Android, iOS, and other platforms. In a later section, we will use these code snippets, but for now, let's just add the user identification functionality to our Lambda functions.

So head back to the editor and update the `model.js` file, because the user that created and updated the articles must be identified:

```
const uuid = require('uuid');
class Article{
    constructor(id, user_id, text) {
        this.article_id = id;
        this.text = text;
        this.user_id = user-id;
    }
}
const createArticle = (event, context, callback) => {
```

```
        validateAttributes(event, callback);
        const body = JSON.parse(event.body);
        const id = uuid.v1();
        const text = body.text;
        const user-id = context.identity.cognitoIdentityId;
        return new Article(id, user_id, text);
    }
```

We will add a new property, `user_id`, to the constructor. The user ID can be taken from Cognito. We will access an object that we haven't used so far-the context object. If our Lambda function has been called for a request that is authenticated or that uses the Cognito pool for identification, then the context object will have an identity property named `cognitoIdentityId`. Once this is done, add it to our constructor. We also do the same with the `updateArticle` method. The `deleteArticle` and `readArticle` methods can stay as they are, but we now need to invoke our `createArticle` method differently:

```
'use strict';
const AWS = require('aws-sdk');
const dynamo = new AWS.DynamoDB.DocumentClient();
const createArticle = require('./model.js').createArticle;
const DynamoDAO = require('../util/dynamo-dao.js');
const ArticleController = require('./controller.js');
module.exports.handler = (event, context, callback) => {
    const article = createArticle(event, context, callback);
    const dynamoDAO = new DynamoDAO(dynamo, 'BlogTable');
    const controller = new ArticleController(dynamoDAO);
    controller.createArticle(article, callback);
};
```

The same applies for our `update` method:

```
'use strict';
const AWS = require('aws-sdk');
const dynamo = new AWS.DynamoDB.DocumentClient();
const updateArticle = require('./model.js').updateArticle;
const DynamoDAO = require('../util/dynamo-dao.js');
const ArticleController = require('./controller.js');
module.exports.handler = (event, context, callback) => {
    const article = updateArticle(event, context, callback);
    const dynamoDAO = new DynamoDAO(dynamo, 'BlogTable');
    const controller = new ArticleController(dynamoDAO);
    controller.updateArticle(article, callback);
};
```

Let us now deploy the frontend to CloudFront and then try out the full stack application.

Deploying a serverless frontend on CloudFront

We are going to take a look at deploying our serverless application frontend to Amazon S3. Then we will deploy our frontend to edge locations on CloudFront. Last but not least, we will benchmark the latency of our frontend.

So let's get started!

Create an S3 bucket named `sls-frontend` in the S3 dashboard on the AWS Management Console. To upload data to the bucket, click on the **Upload** button and drag your local web directory into the bucket:

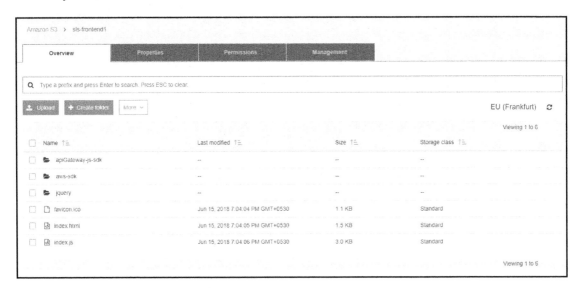

As you can see from the previous screenshot, once the files are uploaded, we need to specify that our bucket is used for static website hosting, so we enable website hosting, set it as an index HTML document, and click on **Save**:

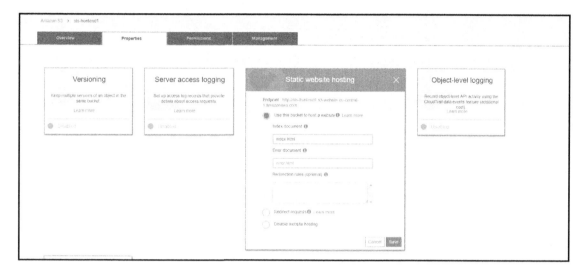

We also need to get some permissions so that our website will be accessible from the internet and other users will be able to access it. We specify that S3:GetObject actions are allowed on our bucket where we host our frontend. Click on **Save**:

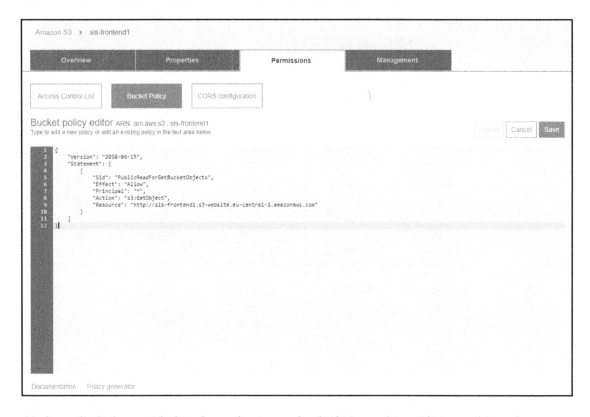

Click on the link provided in the endpoint to check if it's working. If it's working, then you should see the following:

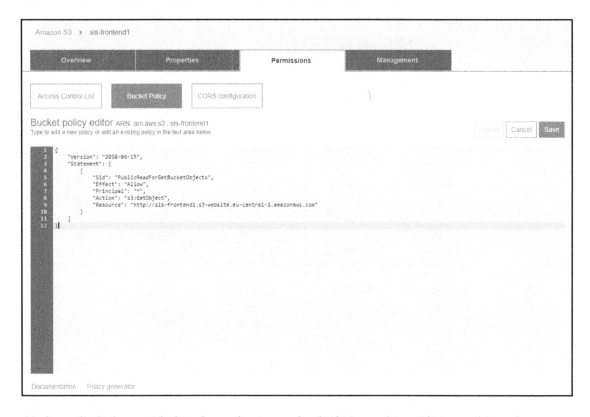

Hello World

As seen in the preceding screenshot, the website will say **Hello World**.

Take a look at the developer console and you will notice the response from the create object request that we make.

Take a look at the speed test of our website:

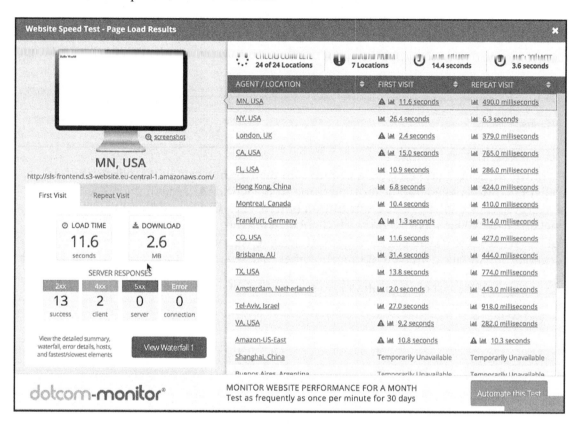

You will notice that, not surprisingly, the performance in Europe is quite good compared to other locations.

There are also some errors. These arise because the permissions have not been updated in the other regions yet, which is a process that can take a little more time in different regions around the globe. As a result, some of these tests failed because the web clients couldn't access the S3 bucket yet. You will also notice that the repeated visit is considerably faster, but it's still not quite what we want right now. Let's try to improve that:

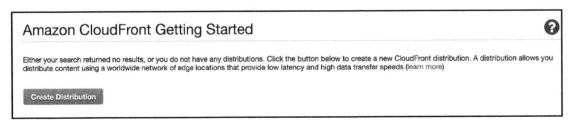

What we are going to do is create a **CloudFront distribution** that will replicate the bucket content in different geographic locations around the world. As seen in the preceding screenshot, click on the **Create Distribution** button, click **Get Started**, and then select the bucket where we have hosted our web client, leaving the other values at their default values. We need to use all edge locations. If needed, we can also select a subset of edge locations. It will take a little bit of time, but after that, we can perform our performance test.

One last configuration is to specify the default root object, which is our index HTML file.

Now access the **CloudFront** distribution at this domain name. We can also use it for our speed testing experiment. Now look at the performance:

This time, our repeated speed test using the CloudFront distribution endpoint shows that performance has significantly improved in at least some regions. In particular, if we look at the United States, the latency is much better than it was before.

There are still some errors, indicating that our permission updates have not propagated to all regions yet, and there are some regions where we have really long latency, so we would need further investigations to find out why that is the case, or maybe give the CloudFront distribution a little bit more time to replicate around the world.

Summary

In this chapter, we built our first serverless application. We used Lambda functions for implementing business logic, DynamoDB for data persistence, Cognito for user identification, and CloudFront for serving the frontend. In the next chapter, you will learn how to program Lambda using other programming languages, in particular Java, Python, and C#.

4
Programming AWS Lambda with Java

Welcome to `Chapter 4`, *Programming AWS Lambda with Java*. In this section, we are going to take a look at using Eclipse and the AWS Eclipse plugin. Then we will program our first Lambda functions with Java. And, last but not least, we will build a simple serverless application using Java. Now let's move on to the first video where we get started with Eclipse and the AWS Eclipse plugin.

In this chapter, we are going to take a look at the following:

- Using Eclipse and the AWS Eclipse plugin
- Programming Lambda functions with Java
- A simple application with Java Lambda functions

So let's dive in!

Getting started with Eclipse and the AWS Eclipse plugin

From this section, you will learn how to install the AWS Eclipse plugin, and also try out some of its features. You will also use the plugin to create our first Java Lambda function.

To find more information about the AWS Toolkit for Eclipse, go to the site of the AWS documentation, which is the open source plugin for the Eclipse IDE. Once you open the site, go over to the left and click on Getting Started and **Set up the Toolkit**.

There, you will find more information, including that you need an AWS account, you need to install Java, and so on. But if you have already installed Java and if you're already using Eclipse, then all you need to do is copy the link `https://aws.amazon.com/eclipse`.

Open your Eclipse IDE. If you have never installed an Eclipse plugin before, there should be a menu action in the menu bar that says **Install New Software**. For macOS, it's under **Help**, but, depending on the operating system, it could be somewhere else. So, find the **Install New Software** menu item and then enter the URL that was copied previously, as shown here:

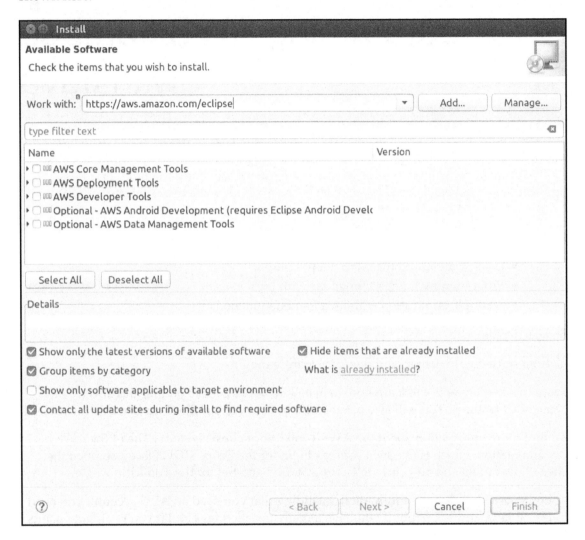

From the previous screenshot, you will find that the AWS Toolkit for Eclipse consists of a bunch of plugins for different AWS services. What we need in this case is the Core plugin, so select the **AWS Toolkit for Eclipse Core** under the **AWS Core Management Tools**. We also need to use the AWS deployment tool for Lambda, so select **AWS Lambda Plugin** under the **AWS Deployment Tools**.

For now, the other plugins are not really needed. Once selected, click on **Next**. This will calculate the dependencies, which should be fine to install. Currently, we am using the Eclipse for Java EE Neon 2 version of Eclipse, but it should work similarly on all major new versions of Eclipse. So, click on **Next**, accept the license agreement, and click on **Finish**. After the software has been installed, we just need to restart Eclipse. Once the Eclipse IDE has restarted, you should see a little orange box, as shown here:

This box will give you more information on how to use the AWS Toolkit for Eclipse if you click on it.

Click on the little drop-down arrow and create a new AWS Lambda Java project:

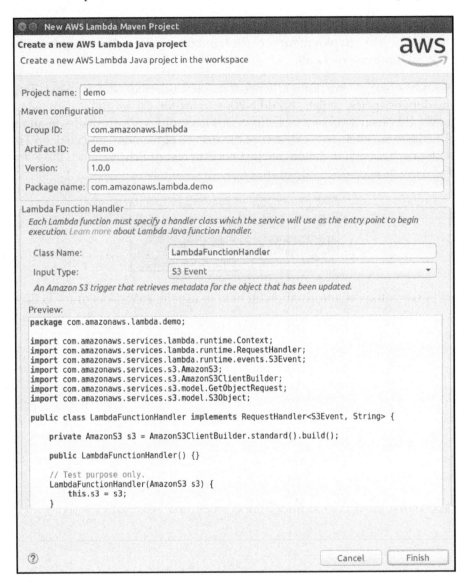

For now, set the **Project Name** as demo. You can also see that we have a group ID and artifact ID, which is used for Maven. And then, at the bottom, you can see that the wizard helps us to generate some boilerplate code.

Let's change the default configuration a little bit. You can choose a different handler type if you want to operate on a stream, but for now let's leave it with a request handler. We could choose a different input type. For a first simple example application, let's use the custom input type. You can see that the code shown in the preview that is generated from our configurations changes. As input type, we could use a plain old Java object, but we could also use something such as a string or an integer. So, let's use **Input Type and Output Type as String**, so we can build a really simple *hello-world* application. Let's click on **Finish**.

When we have created our AWS Lambda Java project, there will be more information on how to get started. But, in our example IDE configuration, there are a couple of problems that are pointed out, as follows:

These errors might not even happen in your case, but, in case they appear, let's see on how to fix them.

In the preceding screenshot, the problem is that the build path was not configured correctly. The reason is because of using the outdated Java version 1.5. We need to change that. So, go to the project explorer tab, click on demo, and go to **demo** | **Build Path** | **Configure Build path**:

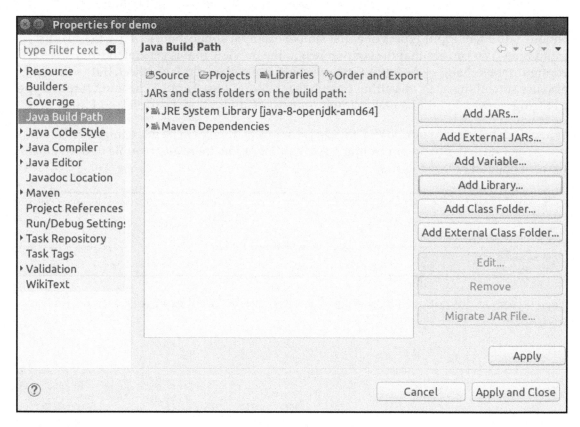

As shown in the preceding screenshot, you will see that Java version is 1.5, so change it by clicking on Add Library. Choose a different JRE system library, namely Java SE8, and click on **Finish**. Once done, remove the Java 1.5 and click on **OK**.

This has not solved all the problems yet. We also need to make sure that the project properties are set correctly. So, go back to the **Build Path** and go to the **Java Compiler**:

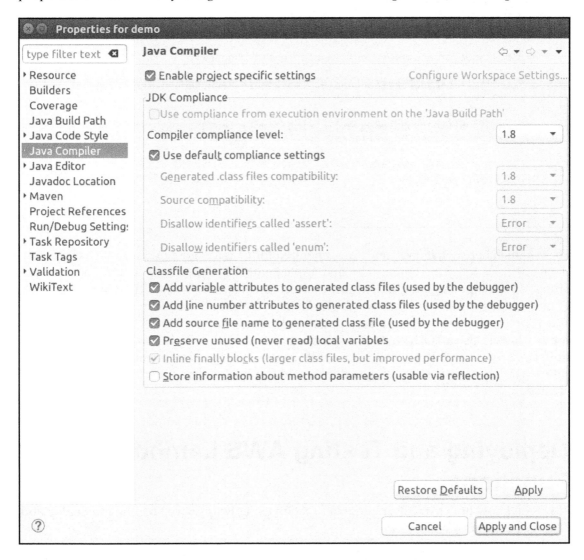

In the preceding screenshot, you'll notice that the compliance level is set to Java 1.8, but we need to use Java 1.8. Click on **OK** and rebuild. This will remove all the errors.

OK, let's take a quick look at the `LambdaFunctionHandler`:

```
LambdaFunctionHandler.java ⊠   demo/pom.xml      LambdaFunctionHandlerTest.java
 1  package com.amazonaws.lambda.demo;
 2
 3⊕import com.amazonaws.services.lambda.runtime.Context;
 5
 6  public class LambdaFunctionHandler implements RequestHandler<String, String> {
 7
 8⊕     @Override
 9      public String handleRequest(String input, Context context) {
10          context.getLogger().log("Input: " + input);
11
12          // TODO: implement your handler
13          return input;
14      }
15  }
```

So, as shown here, what has been auto-generated for us is a class, which is a Java class with the name `LambdaFunctionHandler` that implements the request handler interface, using a string as both input and output. A context object can also be accessed. Right now, our Lambda function handler is pretty simple. There is the `handleRequest` function, which takes two parameters, a string-type input, and the context object, which just logs out the input. There is also a TODO, which implements your handler. Right now, it just returns null. If we return an integer, it won't compile because the handler function is supposed to return a string. Now we are going to deploy and test the Lambda function that we have just created.

Deploying and Testing AWS Lambda Functions

Now you know how to create a Lambda function using Eclipse, we are going to deploy and test our function.

First, we will set up our Eclipse IDE with AWS credentials so that we can access AWS from within Eclipse. Then we will deploy and run our Lambda function from within Eclipse. And, last but not least, we will take a look at the Lambda function on our AWS Management Console.

Go back to the Eclipse IDE. The first thing that we need to check before we can upload and run our Lambda function is if Eclipse has access credentials to access AWS. So, open the **Preferences** and you can see on the left-hand side there is an item for **AWS Toolkit**, as shown in the following screenshot:

As you can see in the preceding screenshot, the Toolkit is set up with the default AWS profile, including the access key ID and the secret access key.

> **TIP**
>
> If you have set up an AWS credentials file on your local file system, Eclipse will take the information from that file. Otherwise, you need to enter it. Please go back to the install and setup guide if this has not been set up for your Eclipse IDE.

Now let's deploy our Lambda function. Go to the demo project folder and click on **Amazon Web Services**, as shown here:

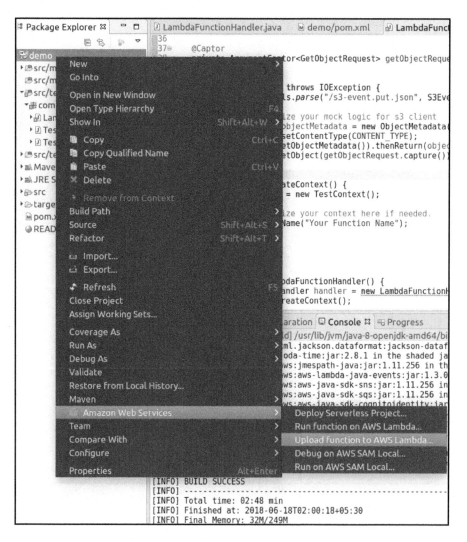

You can see that there are three different options: deploying the project, running a function, and **Upload function to AWS Lambda**.

The first thing that we need to do is upload our function to Lambda:

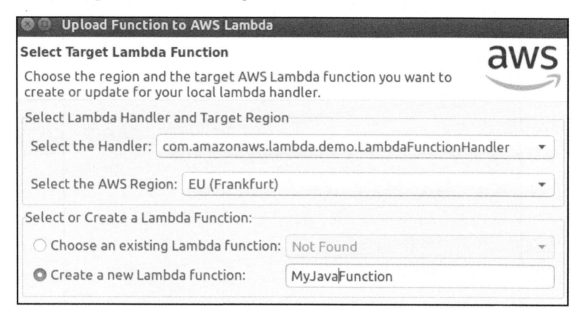

Select the region and name the function `MyJavaFunction`.

Click on **Next**.

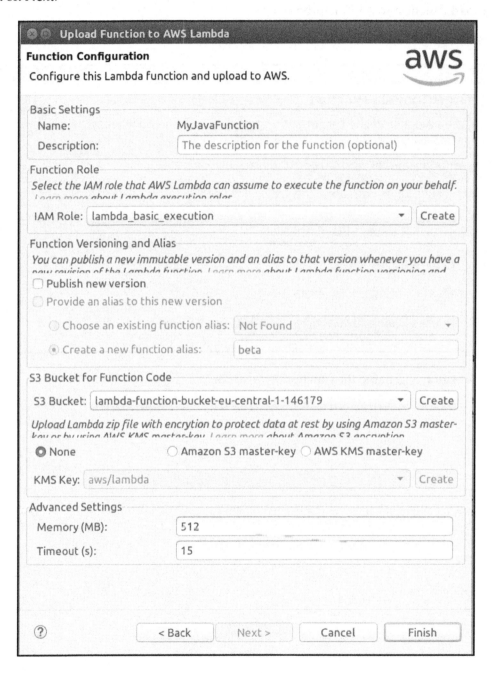

As shown in the preceding screenshot, there are some more configurations that can be made, such as the IAM role, where you can use the Lambda basic execution role or you can create a new role. You can select a bucket where you want to store the function codes for the Java class files and dependencies, and also select how much memory you want to give the Lambda function. For now, let's go over to default settings and click on **Finish**. This will upload the code to the S3 bucket to create the new Lambda function.

Once the Lambda function has been uploaded, run it. Go to **AWS Web Services** and click on the option **Run Function on AWS Lambda**. We need to enter some input and invoke the function. So, let's enter a JSON input and then invoke the Lambda function. The function that we have created expects a string as input, so give it a string and click on **Invoke**. What you will see is that our function output is Hello World, as shown here:

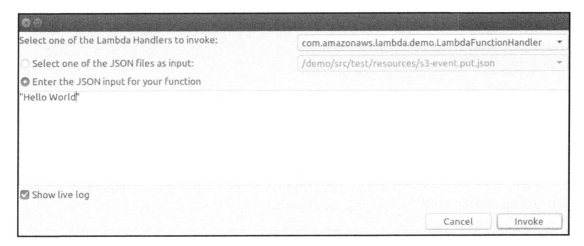

Now let's move on to the AWS Lambda dashboard on the AWS Management Console:

	Function name ▼	Description	Runtime ▼	Code size ▼	Last Modified ▼
○	blog-dev-deleteArticle		Node.js 4.3	6.5 MB	Fri Jun 15 2018 17:54:53 GMT+0530 (IST)
○	blog-dev-updateArticle		Node.js 4.3	6.5 MB	Fri Jun 15 2018 17:54:52 GMT+0530 (IST)
○	greeterHelloWorldSkill	Please use alexa-skills-kit-nodejs-factskill from the Serverless Application Repository	Node.js 6.10	179.5 kB	Thu Jun 07 2018 13:11:57 GMT+0530 (IST)
○	HelloWorld	A starter AWS Lambda function.	Python 2.7	259 bytes	Thu Jun 14 2018 16:10:29 GMT+0530 (IST)
○	MyJavaFunction		Java 8	16.1 MB	Mon Jun 18 2018 02:51:07 GMT+0530 (IST)
○	blog-dev-createArticle		Node.js 4.3	6.5 MB	Fri Jun 15 2018 17:54:52 GMT+0530 (IST)
○	blog-dev-readArticle		Node.js 4.3	6.5 MB	Fri Jun 15 2018 17:54:52 GMT+0530 (IST)
○	handsFreeMesssengerSkill	Please use alexa-skills-kit-nodejs-factskill from the Serverless Application Repository	Node.js 6.10	179.5 kB	Thu Jun 07 2018 13:05:02 GMT+0530 (IST)
○	firstLambda1		Node.js 4.3	216 bytes	Wed Jun 06 2018 16:40:40 GMT+0530 (IST)
○	123		Node.js 4.3	229 bytes	Wed Jun 06 2018 16:09:23 GMT+0530 (IST)

As you can see in the preceding screenshot, the **MyJavaFunction Lambda** function has been added using **Java 8** at runtime. If you click on the function, you can see some more information, such as configuration details, triggers, and monitoring data. You can also see the logs by clicking on **View logs** in CloudWatch:

Time (UTC +00:00)	Message
2018-06-17	
	No older events found at the moment. Retry.
▸ 21:21:08	START RequestId: 599b9004-7274-11e8-b84f-fd2e27562690 Version: $LATEST
▸ 21:21:08	Input: Hello World
▸ 21:21:08	END RequestId: 599b9004-7274-11e8-b84f-fd2e27562690
▸ 21:21:08	REPORT RequestId: 599b9004-7274-11e8-b84f-fd2e27562690 Duration: 49.79 ms Billed Duration: 100 ms Memory Size: 512 MB Max Memory Used: 41 MB
▸ 21:31:08	START RequestId: bf657ee4-7275-11e8-a86c-bfea079c3265 Version: $LATEST
▸ 21:31:08	Input: random string
▸ 21:31:08	END RequestId: bf657ee4-7275-11e8-a86c-bfea079c3265
▸ 21:31:08	REPORT RequestId: bf657ee4-7275-11e8-a86c-bfea079c3265 Duration: 2.29 ms Billed Duration: 100 ms Memory Size: 512 MB Max Memory Used: 41 MB
	No newer events found at the moment. Retry.

As you can see in the preceding screenshot, there is a new log stream for the Lambda function and it also states `Input: random string`.

Now let's access the context object and return some of the runtime information of our Lambda function. Go back to the Eclipse IDE and edit the code to access the context object. For example, we could return the remaining time in milliseconds. This is an integer, so let's make it into a string, as shown here:

```java
LambdaFunctionHandler.java ⊠   demo/pom.xml      LambdaFunctionHandlerTest.java

 1 package com.amazonaws.lambda.demo;
 2
 3 import com.amazonaws.services.lambda.runtime.Context;
 5
 6 public class LambdaFunctionHandler implements RequestHandler<String, String> {
 7
 8     @Override
 9     public String handleRequest(String input, Context context) {
10         context.getLogger().log("Input: " + input);
11
12         // TODO: implement your handler
13         return "Remaining time [ms]: " + context.getRemainingTimeInMillis();
14     }
15 }
```

Next, we run our function again, and, since our code has changed, it must first upload the new function code to `MyJavaFunction`:

```
Problems   Javadoc   Declaration   Console ⊠   Progress
com.amazonaws.lambda.demo.LambdaFunctionHandler Lambda Console
Uploading function code to MyJavaFunction...
Upload success. Function ARN: arn:aws:lambda:eu-central-1:019859648260:function:MyJavaFunction
Invoking function...
================= FUNCTION OUTPUT ===================
"Remaining time [ms]: 14966"
================= FUNCTION LOG OUTPUT ===============
START RequestId: 84fab445-7276-11e8-88bc-bdf9fa9c4f31 Version: $LATEST
Input: random stringEND RequestId: 84fab445-7276-11e8-88bc-bdf9fa9c4f31
REPORT RequestId: 84fab445-7276-11e8-88bc-bdf9fa9c4f31  Duration: 37.89 ms    Billed Duration: 100 ms    Memory Size: 512 MB    Max Memory Used: 41 MB
```

Now the function has been invoked, and, as you can see, the remaining time in milliseconds is 14,976 milliseconds. So, our default configuration of the Lambda function is 15 seconds.

Let's now to build a slightly more complex Lambda function that takes an S3 event as input.

Lambda Function with S3 Event Input

Previously, we created a synchronous Lambda function that takes the string as input and returns the string as output. Now, we are going to create an asynchronous Lambda function that can be invoked through S3 events, and test the function with a dummy event that can upload a file to S3 and see if the function is triggered by the create-object event.

Open the project that we have created. Let's add a new Lambda function handler to the project. Click on the little orange box and select **New AWS Lambda Function**. We will create a new function handler name, S3FunctionHandler; use the default input type that is already selected, S3 Event; and as leave the output type as object:

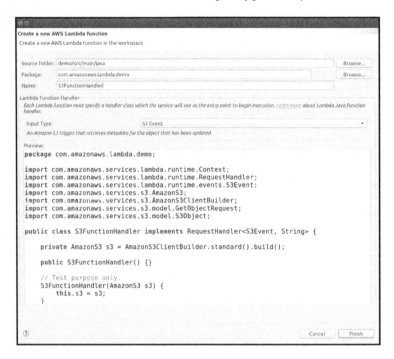

Click on **Finish**. This will create some boilerplate code with the Lambda function handler that takes an S3 event as input:

```
LambdaFunctionHandler.java   S3FunctionHandler.java
 1 package com.amazonaws.lambda.demo;
 2
 3 import com.amazonaws.services.lambda.runtime.Context;
 8
 9 public class S3FunctionHandler implements RequestHandler<S3Event, Object> {
10
11     @Override
12     public Object handleRequest(S3Event input, Context context) {
13         context.getLogger().log("Input: " + input);
14
15         // TODO: implement your handler
16         return null;
17     }
18 }
```

Let's deploy the new function. Right click on demo and go to **Amazon Web Services |
Upload function to AWS Lambda**.

You will notice that the region is still EU Central in Frankfurt, but, instead, we create a new
Lambda function, `MyS3JavaFunction`. Click on `Next`. There will be two Lambda function
handlers. Since we don't want to deploy the same Lambda function as before, let's deploy
the new function handler that we've just created. Select `S3FunctionHandler` and select an
IAM Role:

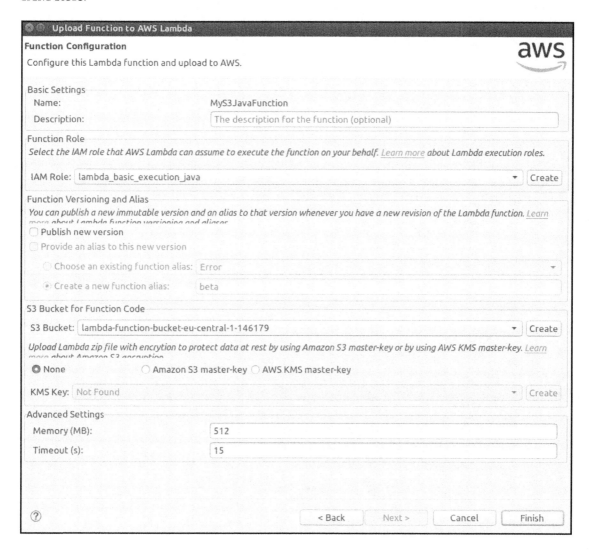

Click on **Finish** to upload the code.

Once the code has been uploaded, we switch over to the AWS Management Console to test our Lambda function with a dummy S3 event. You will notice that, on the Management Console, we have selected **MyS3JavaFunction**. We need to test it, so to do this let's configure a test event. Select the **S3 Put event**, which you find by clicking on the **Actions** tab. This simulates somebody uploading a new object to an S3 bucket. Click on **Save and Test**. The Lambda function returns null and the log output here is the S3 event, as follows:

When you go back to the **Eclipse IDE**, you will see that the input event is not very verbose. We need to give out some more information about our S3 event. Make the console output a little bit more verbose by replacing the code with the following:

```java
package com.amazonaws.lambda.demo;

import com.amazonaws.services.lambda.runtime.Context;

public class S3FunctionHandler implements RequestHandler<S3Event, Object> {

    @Override
    public Object handleRequest(S3Event input, Context context) {
        for(S3EventNotificationRecord rec : input.getRecords()) {
            context.getLogger().log("Event Name: " + rec.getEventName() + "\n");
            context.getLogger().log("Event Source: " + rec.getEventSource() + "\n");
            S3ObjectEntity s3object = rec.getS3().getObject();
            context.getLogger().log("S3 Object Key: " + s3object.getKey() + "\n");
        }

        // TODO: implement your handler
        return null;
    }
}
```

We need to iterate over the records, which are of the type **S3EventNotificationRecord**. Then we'll output some information, such as the event name, the event source, and the object that has triggered the event. Now let's update our code by choosing the same function as before, by clicking **Next** and **Finish** to upload the code. Once the function has been updated, we will head back to our AWS Management Console.

Go to the AWS Lambda dashboard and click on the **Test** button again.

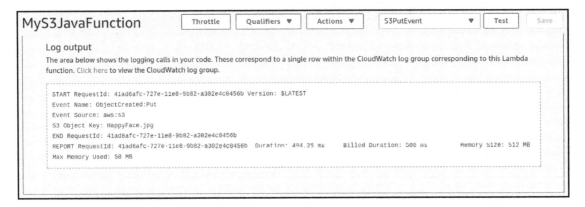

As you can see, it uses the same dummy event from before and the log statements can be seen; for example, the event name, which is the ObjectCreated event of type put. The Event Source is S3 and the object key is HappyFace.jpg.

So now we know that the Lambda function can process S3 events. How about testing it with a real S3 event?

Click on the **Triggers** tab and add a new trigger to our Lambda function. You can select from a number of triggers, but we want to choose the S3 trigger. Let's use the S3 bucket that has been created previously. If you don't have an S3 bucket yet, create a bucket and then we'll test our Lambda function with events in the bucket. We can also specify which type of events we want to trigger our Lambda function. We will go for **Object Created** events and click on **Submit**. This will create a trigger for the Lambda function, as shown here:

Let's go to the **S3** dashboard, upload a file into our S3 bucket, and then check if we can see the metadata of the file that we have uploaded in the log statements of our Lambda function.

Go to the **S3** dashboard and upload a file into the bucket that has the created trigger. Once the file has been uploaded, take a look at the Lambda log. Go back to the dashboard of the Lambda function, and click on **Monitoring and View logs** in CloudWatch. As you can see in the following logs, we have our dummy event, the `HappyFace.jpg` file, but we also have the `Smiling-Cat.jpg` that we have just uploaded:

Filter events		all 2018-06-17 (15.00:00) - 2018-06-18 (15:00:00) ▾
Time (UTC +00:00)	**Message**	**Show in stream**
2018-06-17		
	No older events found for the selected date range. Adjust the date range.	
22:09:34	START RequestId: 1d95081e-727b-11e8-bc22-d3d366b63e30 Version: $LATEST	☐ 2018/06/17/[$LATEST]2ffed0e7cea2…
22:09:35	Input: com.amazonaws.services.lambda.runtime.events.S3Event@bd8db5a	☐ 2018/06/17/[$LATEST]2ffed0e7cea2…
22:09:35	END RequestId: 1d95081e-727b-11e8-bc22-d3d366b63e30	☐ 2018/06/17/[$LATEST]2ffed0e7cea2…
22:09:35	REPORT RequestId: 1d95081e-727b-11e8-bc22-d3d366b63e30 Duration: 610.74 ms Billed Duration: 700 ms Memory	☐ 2018/06/17/[$LATEST]2ffed0e7cea2…
22:14:45	START RequestId: d7915635-727b-11e8-a75d-b33a8a9a98f9 Version: $LATEST	☐ 2018/06/17/[$LATEST]2ffed0e7cea2…
22:14:45	Input: com.amazonaws.services.lambda.runtime.events.S3Event@7a187f14	☐ 2018/06/17/[$LATEST]2ffed0e7cea2…
22:14:45	END RequestId: d7915635-727b-11e8-a75d-b33a8a9a98f9	☐ 2018/06/17/[$LATEST]2ffed0e7cea2…
22:14:45	REPORT RequestId: d7915635-727b-11e8-a75d-b33a8a9a98f9 Duration: 40.49 ms Billed Duration: 100 ms Memory S	☐ 2018/06/17/[$LATEST]cf952b199cf5…
22:32:03	START RequestId: 41ad6afc-727e-11e8-9b82-a302e4c0456b Version: $LATEST	☐ 2018/06/17/[$LATEST]cf952b199cf5…
22:32:04	Event Name: ObjectCreated:Put	☐ 2018/06/17/[$LATEST]cf952b199cf5…
22:32:04	Event Source: aws:s3	☐ 2018/06/17/[$LATEST]cf952b199cf5…
22:32:04	S3 Object Key: HappyFace.jpg	☐ 2018/06/17/[$LATEST]ef952b199cf5…
22:32:04	END RequestId: 41ad6afc-727e-11e8-9b82-a302e4c0456b	☐ 2018/06/17/[$LATEST]cf952b199cf5…
22:32:04	REPORT RequestId: 41ad6afc-727e-11e8-9b82-a302e4c0456b Duration: 494.25 ms Billed Duration: 500 ms Memory	☐ 2018/06/17/[$LATEST]cf952b199cf5…
2018-06-18		
14:24:09	START RequestId: 43666431-7303-11e8-8b35-e3e8e3789dfc Version: $LATEST	☐ 2018/06/18/[$LATEST]bcbe2b289dc…
14:24:10	Event Name: ObjectCreated:Put	☐ 2018/06/18/[$LATEST]bcbe2b289dc…
14:24:10	Event Source: aws:s3	☐ 2018/06/18/[$LATEST]bcbe2b289dc…
14:24:10	S3 Object Key: smiling-cat.jpg	☐ 2018/06/18/[$LATEST]bcbe2b289dc…
14:24:10	END RequestId: 43666431-7303-11e8-8b35-e3e8e3789dfc	☐ 2018/06/18/[$LATEST]bcbe2b289dc…
14:24:10	REPORT RequestId: 43666431-7303-11e8-8b35-e3e8e3789dfc Duration: 757.83 ms Billed Duration: 800 ms Memory	☐ 2018/06/18/[$LATEST]bcbe2b289dc…
	No newer events found for the selected date range. Adjust the date range.	

As you can imagine, you can do a lot of things with the Lambda function using triggers. For example, we could process the JPEG file, transform it into a thumbnail, store that thumbnail into another S3 bucket, and then load it onto your Web page to load faster. As you can imagine, you could do a lot of things with this Lambda function.

Creating a Simple Serverless Java Project

Now we will create a serverless project that uses Lambda functions in combination with other AWS services. For this purpose, we are going to use the AWS Toolkit plugin in Eclipse to create a serverless project from a project blueprint. We will take a look at the source code and template files that are created in this project, and then we will deploy and test the application.

Open the Eclipse IDE and click on the little orange AWS icon to create a new AWS serverless project. Let's give it the project name `JavaBlog` and select the article blueprint. You can have a look at the files that have been created for in the `JavaBlog` project, as shown here:

As you can see, there are two articles: `GetArticle` and `PutArticle`. Let's have a look at the put article Lambda function first:

```java
PutArticle.java ⊠
 1 package com.serverless.demo.function;
 2
 3 import java.io.ByteArrayInputStream;
25
26 /**
27  * Lambda function that triggered by the API Gateway event "POST /". It reads all the query parameters as the metadata for this
28  * article and stores them to a DynamoDB table. It reads the payload as the content of the article and stores it to a S3 bucket.
29  */
30 public class PutArticle implements RequestHandler<ServerlessInput, ServerlessOutput> {
31     // DynamoDB table name for storing article metadata.
32     private static final String ARTICLE_TABLE_NAME = System.getenv("ARTICLE_TABLE_NAME");
33     // DynamoDB table attribute name for storing article id.
34     private static final String ARTICLE_TABLE_ID_NAME = "id";
35     // DynamoDB table attribute name for storing the bucket name where holds the article's content.
36     private static final String ARTICLE_TABLE_BUCKET_NAME = "bucket";
37     // DynamoDB table attribute name for storing the bucket object key name that contains the article's content.
38     private static final String ARTICLE_TABLE_KEY_NAME = "key";
39     // S3 bucket name for storing article content.
40     private static final String ARTICLE_BUCKET_NAME = System.getenv("ARTICLE_BUCKET_NAME");
41     @Override
42     public ServerlessOutput handleRequest(ServerlessInput serverlessInput, Context context) {
43             // Using builder to create the clients could allow us to dynamically load the region from the AWS_REGION environment
44             // variable. Therefore we can deploy the Lambda functions to different regions without code change.
45             AmazonDynamoDB dynamoDb = AmazonDynamoDBClientBuilder.standard().build();
46             AmazonS3 s3 = AmazonS3ClientBuilder.standard().build();
47             ServerlessOutput output = new ServerlessOutput();
48
49             try {
50                 String keyName = UUID.randomUUID().toString();
51                 String content = serverlessInput.getBody();
52                 s3.putObject(new PutObjectRequest(
53                         ARTICLE_BUCKET_NAME,
54                         keyName,
55                         new ByteArrayInputStream(content.getBytes(StandardCharsets.UTF_8)),
56                         new ObjectMetadata())
57                 );
58
59                 Map<String, AttributeValue> attributes = convert(serverlessInput.getQueryStringParameters());
60                 attributes.putIfAbsent(ARTICLE_TABLE_ID_NAME, new AttributeValue().withS(UUID.randomUUID().toString()));
61                 attributes.put(ARTICLE_TABLE_BUCKET_NAME, new AttributeValue().withS(ARTICLE_BUCKET_NAME));
62                 attributes.put(ARTICLE_TABLE_KEY_NAME, new AttributeValue().withS(keyName));
63                 dynamoDb.putItem(new PutItemRequest()
64                         .withTableName(ARTICLE_TABLE_NAME)
65                         .withItem(attributes));
66                 output.setStatusCode(200);
```

As you can see in the previous comments, the Lambda function is supposed to be created by a HTTP post request through an API Gateway. We'll read the metadata from our HTTP request and store that metadata in a DynamoDB table record. Then we'll take the payload from our post body and store the payload in a S3 object in a S3 bucket. The table name, the table schema, the bucket name, and so on are specified here:

```java
// DynamoDB table name for storing article metadata.
private static final String ARTICLE_TABLE_NAME = System.getenv("ARTICLE_TABLE_NAME");
// DynamoDB table attribute name for storing article id.
private static final String ARTICLE_TABLE_ID_NAME = "id";
// DynamoDB table attribute name for storing the bucket name where holds the article's content.
private static final String ARTICLE_TABLE_BUCKET_NAME = "bucket";
// DynamoDB table attribute name for storing the bucket object key name that contains the article's content.
private static final String ARTICLE_TABLE_KEY_NAME = "key";
// S3 bucket name for storing article content.
private static final String ARTICLE_BUCKET_NAME = System.getenv("ARTICLE_BUCKET_NAME");
@Override
public ServerlessOutput handleRequest(ServerlessInput serverlessInput, Context context) {
        // Using builder to create the clients could allow us to dynamically load the region from the AWS_REGION envir
        // variable. Therefore we can deploy the Lambda functions to different regions without code change.
        AmazonDynamoDB dynamoDb = AmazonDynamoDBClientBuilder.standard().build();
        AmazonS3 s3 = AmazonS3ClientBuilder.standard().build();
        ServerlessOutput output = new ServerlessOutput();

        try {
            String keyName = UUID.randomUUID().toString();
            String content = serverlessInput.getBody();
            s3.putObject(new PutObjectRequest(
                    ARTICLE_BUCKET_NAME,
                    keyName,
                    new ByteArrayInputStream(content.getBytes(StandardCharsets.UTF_8)),
                    new ObjectMetadata())
            );

            Map<String, AttributeValue> attributes = convert(serverlessInput.getQueryStringParameters());
            attributes.putIfAbsent(ARTICLE_TABLE_ID_NAME, new AttributeValue().withS(UUID.randomUUID().toString()));
            attributes.put(ARTICLE_TABLE_BUCKET_NAME, new AttributeValue().withS(ARTICLE_BUCKET_NAME));
            attributes.put(ARTICLE_TABLE_KEY_NAME, new AttributeValue().withS(keyName));
            dynamoDb.putItem(new PutItemRequest()
```

If we scroll down to the Lambda function handler, we can see that it takes an object of type `serverlessInput` as input. And, in return, it expects a `serverlessOutput` object, which you can see in the following screenshot:

These objects basically wrap around the HTTP requests. For example, in the
ServerlessInput, our input has a body of headers, queryStringParameters, and so
on:

```java
package com.serverless.demo.model;

import java.util.Map;

public class ServerlessInput {

    private String resource;
    private String path;
    private String httpMethod;
    private Map<String, String> headers;
    private Map<String, String> queryStringParameters;
    private Map<String, String> pathParameters;
    private Map<String, String> stageVariables;
    private String body;
    private RequestContext requestContext;
    private Boolean isBase64Encoded;

    public String getResource() {
        return resource;
    }
    public void setResource(String resource) {
        this.resource = resource;
    }
    public ServerlessInput withResource(String resource) {
        setResource(resource);
        return this;
    }
    public String getPath() {
        return path;
    }
    public void setPath(String path) {
        this.path = path;
    }
    public ServerlessInput withPath(String path) {
        setPath(path);
        return this;
    }
    public String getHttpMethod() {
```

So, let's go back to the put article Lambda function handler and see what it does:

```
42    public ServerlessOutput handleRequest(ServerlessInput serverlessInput, Context context) {
43        // Using builder to create the clients could allow us to dynamically load the region from the AWS_REGION envi
44        // variable. Therefore we can deploy the Lambda functions to different regions without code change.
45        AmazonDynamoDB dynamoDb = AmazonDynamoDBClientBuilder.standard().build();
46        AmazonS3 s3 = AmazonS3ClientBuilder.standard().build();
47        ServerlessOutput output = new ServerlessOutput();
48
49        try {
50            String keyName = UUID.randomUUID().toString();
51            String content = serverlessInput.getBody();
52            s3.putObject(new PutObjectRequest(
53                ARTICLE_BUCKET_NAME,
54                keyName,
55                new ByteArrayInputStream(content.getBytes(StandardCharsets.UTF_8)),
56                new ObjectMetadata())
57            );
58
59            Map<String, AttributeValue> attributes = convert(serverlessInput.getQueryStringParameters());
60            attributes.putIfAbsent(ARTICLE_TABLE_ID_NAME, new AttributeValue().withS(UUID.randomUUID().toString()));
61            attributes.put(ARTICLE_TABLE_BUCKET_NAME, new AttributeValue().withS(ARTICLE_BUCKET_NAME));
62            attributes.put(ARTICLE_TABLE_KEY_NAME, new AttributeValue().withS(keyName));
63            dynamoDb.putItem(new PutItemRequest()
64                .withTableName(ARTICLE_TABLE_NAME)
```

The first things that you can see in the preceding screenshot are the instantiated DynamoDB client and Amazon S3 client. We already prepared the `ServerlessOutput` object that we return through our synchronous function location:

```
AmazonDynamoDB dynamoDb = AmazonDynamoDBClientBuilder.standard().build();
AmazonS3 s3 = AmazonS3ClientBuilder.standard().build();
```

Then we create a random UUID, which we use as a key name for our S3 object that we create to start the payload:

```
String keyName = UUID.randomUUID().toString();
String content = serverlessInput.getBody();
s3.putObject(new PutObjectRequest(
        ARTICLE_BUCKET_NAME,
        keyName,
        new ByteArrayInputStream(content.getBytes(StandardCharsets.UTF_8)),
        new ObjectMetadata())
);
```

We read the payload from our `serverlessInput` object, which we retrieve in the function handler, and we execute an S3 `PutObject` request with our article bucket name, which we set up using environment variables. We use the key name with the randomly generated UUID, and as input content we read a `ByteArrayInputStream` from the content that we have retrieved.

So, in the previous piece of code, we store an object, which is the payload of our HTTP post body, in S3 as a new object.

We also store or create a new Dynamo DB record using a `PutItem` request, as shown here:

```
Map<String, AttributeValue> attributes = convert(serverlessInput.getQueryStringParameters());
attributes.putIfAbsent(ARTICLE_TABLE_ID_NAME, new AttributeValue().withS(UUID.randomUUID().toString()));
attributes.put(ARTICLE_TABLE_BUCKET_NAME, new AttributeValue().withS(ARTICLE_BUCKET_NAME));
attributes.put(ARTICLE_TABLE_KEY_NAME, new AttributeValue().withS(keyName));
dynamoDb.putItem(new PutItemRequest()
        .withTableName(ARTICLE_TABLE_NAME)
        .withItem(attributes));
```

The `PutItem` request is performed on a DynamoDB table. The table name is specified using environment variables, and the attributes are specified as shown in the previous screenshot. The attributes specify our hash key, which is the table ID. The previous piece of code will set a randomly generated ID. We're using a string type, and we reference our S3 bucket and the key of our S3 object that we store in the bucket. So, in our DynamoDB table record, you reference the payload that we have stored in Amazon S3.

If we scroll down after we return these two requests, we set the status code on our `ServerlessOutput` object and set the body as a successfully inserted article, as shown here:

```
output.setStatusCode(200);
output.setBody("Successfully inserted article " + attributes.get(ARTICLE_TABLE_ID_NAME).getS());
```

If you take a look at the `GetArticle` function, you will notice that that the `GetArticle` function is supposed to be triggered through an HTTP get event, and it reads the query parameter ID, retrieves the content, returns the content that we have stored in our S3 bucket as a new object, and returns that as payload in our HTTP response.

Now, if we validate our input as shown in the following, we expect to have a query parameter that contains the article table ID name, which is id, and if it is not set, we throw an exception:

```
if (serverlessInput.getQueryStringParameters() == null || serverlessInput.getQueryStringParameters().get(ARTICLE_TABLE_ID_NAME) == null) {
        throw new Exception("Parameter " + ARTICLE_TABLE_ID_NAME + " in query must be provided!");
}
```

If the query parameter is set, then we use it to query our DynamoDB table and we retrieve our item from our DynamoDB record at that ID:

```
Map<String, AttributeValue> item = dynamoDb.getItem(new GetItemRequest()
        .withTableName(ARTICLE_TABLE_NAME)
        .withKey(key))
        .getItem();
```

We retrieve the key of our S3 object from the item that has been returned through our DynamoDB GetItem request:

```
String s3ObjectKey = item.get(ARTICLE_TABLE_KEY_NAME).getS();
```

Once the content has been retrieved, set that content in the serverless output. Another important file that has been generated with our serverless project is the serverless.template file:

```
"Description": "Simple article service.",
"Parameters" : {
  "ArticleBucketName" : {
      "Type" : "String",
      "Default": "serverless-blueprint-article-bucket",
      "Description" : "Name of S3 bucket used to store the article content. If left blank, AWS CloudFormation would manage this resource.",
      "MinLength" : "0"
  },
  "ArticleTableName" : {
      "Type" : "String",
      "Default": "serverless-blueprint-article-table",
      "Description" : "Name of DynamoDB table used to store the article metadata. If left blank, AWS CloudFormation would manage this resource.",
      "MinLength" : "0"
  },
  "ReadCapacity" : {
      "Type" : "Number",
      "Description" : "Read capacity for the DynamoDB blog table.",
      "Default" : "3",
      "MinValue" : 1
  },
  "WriteCapacity" : {
      "Type" : "Number",
      "Description" : "Write capacity for the DynamoDB blog table.",
      "Default" : "3",
      "MinValue" : 1
  }
},
```

Let's take a look at what we find in the previous code in detail. For our application to work, besides our Lambda functions, we also need an S3 bucket and we need a DynamoDB table. You will be able to see some parameters that specify the name of our S3 bucket, the name of our DynamoDB table, and the configurations of our DynamoDB table.

Below the template, we can see some resources that get set up through this template:

```
"GetArticle": {
  "Type": "AWS::Serverless::Function",
  "Properties": {
    "Handler": "com.serverless.demo.function.GetArticle",
    "Runtime" : "java8",
    "CodeUri" : "./target/demo-1.0.0.jar",
    "Policies": [
      "AmazonDynamoDBReadOnlyAccess",
      "AmazonS3ReadOnlyAccess"
    ],
    "Environment" : {
      "Variables" : {
        "ARTICLE_TABLE_NAME" : { "Ref" : "ArticleTableName" },
        "ARTICLE_BUCKET_NAME" : { "Ref" : "ArticleBucketName" }
      }
    },
    "Events": {
      "GetResource": {
        "Type": "Api",
        "Properties": {
          "Path": "/",
          "Method": "get"
        }
      }
    }
  }
}
```

First, the GetArticle Lambda function and the Lambda function have a policy that allows our Lambda function to read from the DynamoDB table and our S3 bucket. So, we restrict these policies to our table and our bucket in the application, as shown in the following:

```
"Policies": [
  "AmazonDynamoDBReadOnlyAccess",
  "AmazonS3ReadOnlyAccess"
],
"Environment" : {
  "Variables" : {
    "ARTICLE_TABLE_NAME" : { "Ref" : "ArticleTableName" },
    "ARTICLE_BUCKET_NAME" : { "Ref" : "ArticleBucketName" }
  }
},
```

Now the `PutArticle` function has full DynamoDB access and full Amazon S3 access:

```
"PutArticle": {
  "Type": "AWS::Serverless::Function",
  "Properties": {
    "Handler": "com.serverless.demo.function.PutArticle",
    "Runtime" : "java8",
    "CodeUri" : "./target/demo-1.0.0.jar",
    "Policies": [
      "AmazonDynamoDBFullAccess",
      "AmazonS3FullAccess"
    ],
```

For a production application, you might want to restrict these access rights a little bit further.

Further down, we can see our resource, which specifies our DynamoDB table using the parameters that we have defined previously:

```
"ArticleTable": {
  "Type": "AWS::DynamoDB::Table",
  "Properties": {
    "AttributeDefinitions": [
      {
        "AttributeName": "id",
        "AttributeType": "S"
      }
    ],
    "KeySchema": [
      {
        "AttributeName": "id",
        "KeyType": "HASH"
      }
    ],
    "ProvisionedThroughput": {
      "ReadCapacityUnits": {"Ref" : "ReadCapacity"},
      "WriteCapacityUnits": {"Ref" : "WriteCapacity"}
    },
    "TableName": {"Ref" : "ArticleTableName"}
  }
},
```

And, finally, we can see our `ArticleBucket`, which is using the parameters defined previously:

```
"ArticleBucket": {
    "Type": "AWS::S3::Bucket",
    "Properties": {
        "BucketName": {"Ref" : "ArticleBucketName"}
    }
}
```

OK, now let's upload our serverless project by right-clicking on JavaBlog and going to the **Amazon Web Services | Deployed Serverless Project** button. In this book, we are deploying it in the EU Central region in Frankfurt. This will create a `CloudFormation` stack with the stack name `JavaBlog-devstack`, and then the `CloudFormation` stack will be used to provision the AWS resources, maybe to Lambda functions, the DynamoDB table, and the S3 bucket, with the appropriate policies. Click on **Finish**.

As you can see in the preceding screenshot, our serverless application is being created using the `CloudFormation` stack.

Now, before we deploy our serverless project, we need to change one thing because all S3 bucket names are shared in the global namespace. So, we need to change this bucket name to something else because some other person who uses the AWS Toolkit plugin might have already created this bucket, so we might want to avoid that. For now, we just create a random string of numbers and hope that nobody else has used this bucket name yet:

```
"Default": "serverless-blueprint-article-bucket-23648817236827282",
```

So don't use the exact numbers given here, use something random.

Once you enter, click on the **Java blog and Deploy Serverless Project**. Select the AWS region and use **JavaBlog-devstack** as a **CloudFormation** stack name. Click on **Finish**:

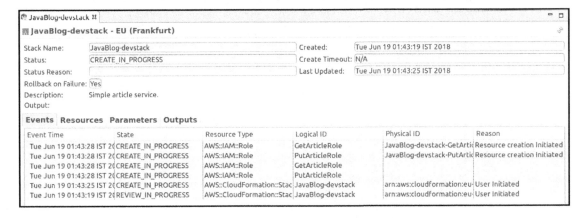

Event Time	State	Resource Type	Logical ID	Physical ID	Reason
Tue Jun 19 01:43:28 IST 2(	CREATE_IN_PROGRESS	AWS::IAM::Role	GetArticleRole	JavaBlog-devstack-GetArtic	Resource creation Initiated
Tue Jun 19 01:43:28 IST 2(	CREATE_IN_PROGRESS	AWS::IAM::Role	PutArticleRole	JavaBlog-devstack-PutArtic	Resource creation Initiated
Tue Jun 19 01:43:28 IST 2(	CREATE_IN_PROGRESS	AWS::IAM::Role	GetArticleRole		
Tue Jun 19 01:43:28 IST 2(	CREATE_IN_PROGRESS	AWS::IAM::Role	PutArticleRole		
Tue Jun 19 01:43:25 IST 2(	CREATE_IN_PROGRESS	AWS::CloudFormation::Stac	JavaBlog-devstack	arn:aws:cloudformation:eu-	User Initiated
Tue Jun 19 01:43:19 IST 2(	REVIEW_IN_PROGRESS	AWS::CloudFormation::Stac	JavaBlog-devstack	arn:aws:cloudformation:eu-	User Initiated

Now the Lambda function code has been uploaded to S3 and our serverless CloudFormation template is used to create the stack of resources that we need-the Lambda functions, `GetArticle` and `PutArticle` functions, the DynamoDB table, the S3 bucket, and the respective IAM policies-so that our Lambda functions are able to access DynamoDB and its three or four read and write operations, respectively.

As you can see in the preceding screenshot, our Lambda functions and the IAM roles of our Lambda functions have been created. Now our Lambda functions are provisioned. Our API Gateway is set up. We have set the permissions. So, basically, all the AWS resources specified in our `serverless.template` file are used to set up and configure our application.

 If your provisioning process has failed, please make sure that you change the bucket name; otherwise, it will fail and the error message will say something like this bucket already exists.

OK, now let's head over to the AWS Management Console. Open the AWS Management Console and on the dashboard of `CloudFormation`, if you scroll further down, there is a new stack, `JavaBlog-devstack`, which has just been created through Eclipse:

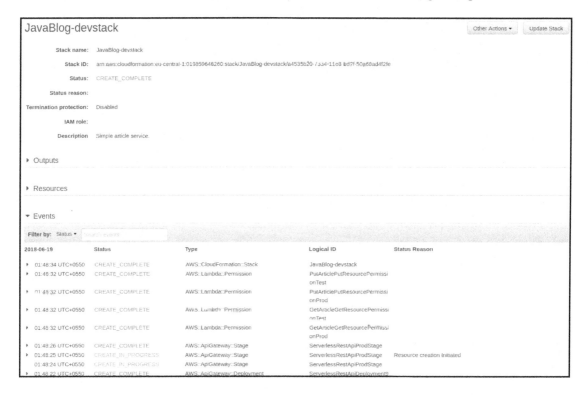

If you click on that, you can see the same information that we have in Eclipse. The operations are processed based on our template. We can also see the template file that was used. Let's take a quick look at the resources that we have provisioned using `CloudFormation`, then let's try it out:

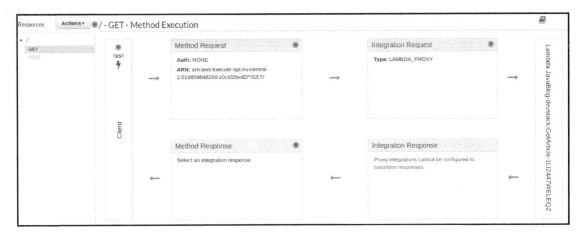

On the API Gateway dashboard, you can see that two HTTP endpoints have been created for get and for post requests, and they are integrated with our Lambda functions. If you click on them, then you can see the Lambda function that has been deployed, as shown in the following screenshot:

If you go to DynamoDB, you can see a new table, `serverless-blueprint-article-table`.

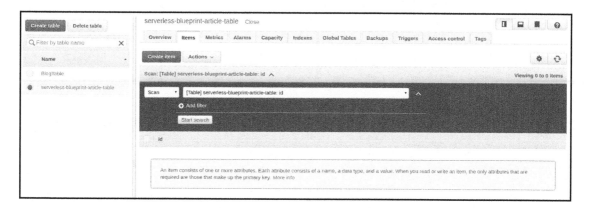

There are no items stored yet. If you go to S3, you can also see the S3 bucket that has been created.

Go back to the API Gateway. You will see the URL endpoint that we can use to test our application, using Postman. Open Postman, paste the URL from our endpoint, and select the post method. We'll make the first request by using simple, plain text, `Hello World`, and pressing **Send**:

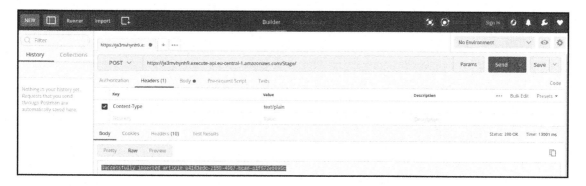

Now as you can see in the previous screenshot, we get back a message that looks like an error, but, actually, if we take a look at the raw message, it says successfully inserted article at ID. So let's do a get request using that ID:

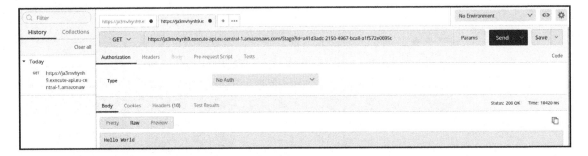

This will return our **Hello World** text. Let's try another attachment for binary, maybe. Attach a JPEG file to your request, which will create another entry in DynamoDB and S3. Let's retrieve it:

Now, if we take a look on our AWS Management Console, we can see two records have been written into DynamoDB which reference the payload in our S3 bucket. And if we look in the S3 bucket, then we can see two objects, as shown here:

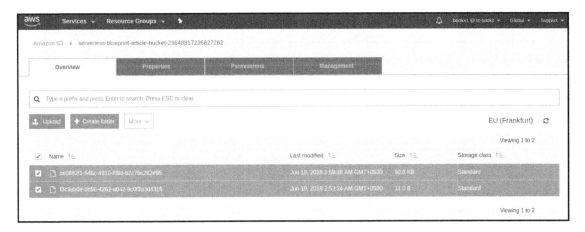

One is the `Hello World` string and the other is the JPEG file.

If we go back to the CloudFormation dashboard, we can take another look at our CloudFormation deployment. We can select **Other Actions** and **View/Edit Templating Designer**. This will open a nice visualization of the resources involved in our project:

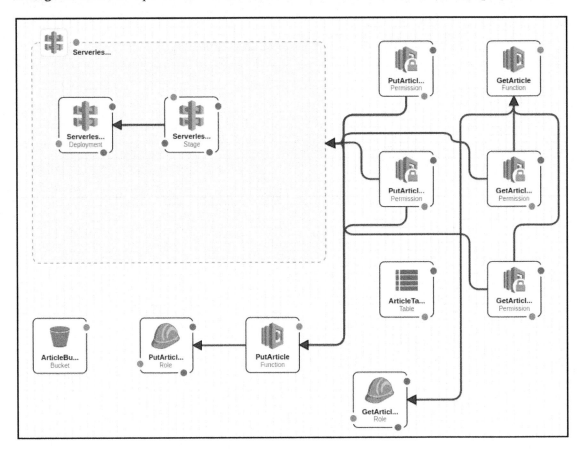

You can also download the image of our deployment. Lastly, close the designer and delete the stack that we have just created, so that we don't have to pay for the provision throughput of our DynamoDB tables. Click on **Actions and Delete Stack**.

Summary

In this chapter, we learned how to use Eclipse with the AWS Toolkit plugin, and we used Java to create and test different Lambda functions. First, we created and tested a Lambda function with a simple string input/output, then a Lambda function that is triggered through S3 events, and, finally, a serverless project that consists of two Lambda functions that write to or read from DynamoDB and S3, respectively. In the next chapter, we are going to take a look how to program AWS Lambda using Python.

Programming AWS Lambda with Python 5

In this chapter, we are going to learn how to program AWS Lambda with Python. In this chapter, we are going to cover the following:

- Creating Python Lambda functions on the AWS Management Console
- Creating Python Lambda functions using the Serverless Framework
- Building a serverless web-application backend with Python

Creating a python lambda function

We are going to use the AWS Management Console to create Python Lambda functions using function blueprints. We will deploy Python functions from the blueprints and then test them.

Sign in to the AWS Management Console and navigate through the AWS Lambda dashboard:

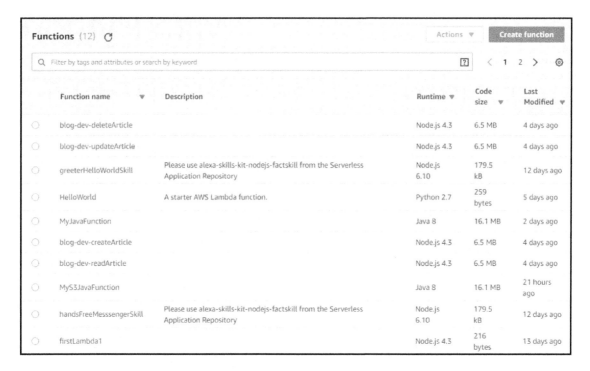

As shown in the preceding screenshot, you can see a list of all the Lambda functions that have already been created throughout this book, most of them in **Node.js** and also some in **Java 8**. Let's create our first Lambda function using Python. Click on **Create a Lambda function**.

We can select the Lambda function from one of the available blueprints provided. Let's start with a simple Blank Function blueprint. Click on the **Blank Function** blueprint. Don't select the trigger and just click **Next**. We need to give our function a name. For now, let's call it PyFun. Select the **Runtime** as well as shown below:

It's now created as Python code. We have a very simple Lambda function handler, which takes two arguments: an event that we invoke our Lambda function with and the context that gives us runtime information on our Lambda function. Let's add another statement that logs the event that we invoke our Lambda function with. Instead of returning Hello from Lambda, return the classic `Hello World`. Scroll down a little bit further, as we need to configure the IAM role that we want to assign to our Lambda function. For now, we use the basic execution role, as shown here:

Scroll down further and click on **Next**. Review the configurations and click on **Create Function**. The following screenshot shows the successfully created function:

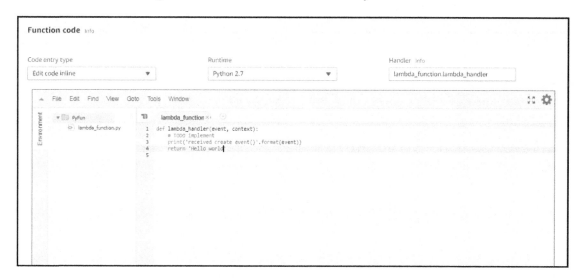

Let's test it with one of the test events. Click on **Configure test events**. We can select whichever of the test events we like. For this chapter, we select the key 3 event. It doesn't really matter; it just prints it out on the console. Scroll down and click **Save and Test**. This will execute or invoke our Lambda function, returning Hello World. We can take a look at this excerpt from the log output, which states the event you have selected.

Let's now go back to the Lambda dashboard, and let's create a more interesting Lambda function from one of the other blueprints. You can select the blueprints by the runtime. How about choosing the **S3 get object type Python** blueprint?

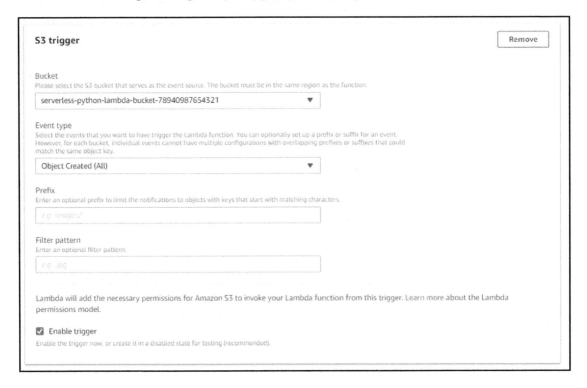

As you can see, a trigger has already been pre-selected. We can also select the Bucket that we want to use. It's Amazon S3 that triggers our Lambda function. So, you can select whichever bucket you want to use. You just need to make sure that a trigger for the Lambda functions on these object-created events doesn't already exist. So, if you are not sure, just create a new bucket. You could also restrict it to listen for only certain events, or for objects that start with a certain prefix or that end with a certain suffix, but, for now, let's leave that empty. What we need to do is click the enable trigger checkbox here, which gives Amazon S3 permission to invoke our Lambda function. Click **Next**.

Now we need to give our Lambda function name. For now, let's name it `PyFunS3`. Let's take a look at the code that has been generated for us using this blueprint:

Lambda function code

Code is pre-configured by the chosen blueprint. You can configure it after you create the function.

Runtime
Python 2.7

```python
1   from __future__ import print_function
2
3   import json
4   import urllib
5   import boto3
6
7   print('Loading function')
8
9   s3 = boto3.client('s3')
10
11
12   def lambda_handler(event, context):
13       #print("Received event: " + json.dumps(event, indent=2))
14
15       # Get the object from the event and show its content type
16       bucket = event['Records'][0]['s3']['bucket']['name']
17       key = urllib.unquote_plus(event['Records'][0]['s3']['object']['key'].encode('utf8'))
18       try:
19           response = s3.get_object(Bucket=bucket, Key=key)
20           print("CONTENT TYPE: " + response['ContentType'])
21           return response['ContentType']
22       except Exception as e:
23           print(e)
24           print('Error getting object {} from bucket {}. Make sure they exist and your bucket is in the same region a
25           raise e
26
```

As you can see here, we import couple of libraries and one of them is the boto library, which you don't need to bundle with your source code because it's already installed on the instance that executes this Lambda function. So, you don't need to download and install this boto dependency. You can just use it by importing it. Here, we create an S3 client using the boto client library:

```
s3 = boto3.client('s3')
```

So, boto is a library used to call Amazon Web Services and, here, we want to call S3 from within our Lambda function. This means our Lambda function is not only triggered by an S3 event, we also want to call the S3 API from within our Lambda function. When our Lambda function is invoked by an S3-object-created event, we are going to do two things:

```
bucket = event['Records'][0]['s3']['bucket']['name']
key = urllib.unquote_plus(event['Records'][0]['s3']['object']['key'].encode('utf8'))
```

We are going to read the bucket in which the object has been created. There could be multiple buckets that trigger the same Lambda function. So, we retrieve the bucket name and retrieve the key name of the object that has been created. Then, we use the boto S3 client to perform a `get_object` request on S3; we retrieve some more information about our object, such as the content type; and then we print out the content type. What we could possibly do here is also retrieve the object content to process it; for example, to create a thumbnail of a bigger picture or to transform a Microsoft Word document into a PDF, or something like that. So, if there's no error, then the content type will be printed out:

```
    response = s3.get_object(Bucket=bucket, Key=key)
    print("CONTENT TYPE: " + response['ContentType'])
    return response['ContentType']
except Exception as e:
    print(e)
    print('Error getting object {} from bucket {}. Make sure they exist and your bucket is in
    raise e
```

Scroll down further to **Lambda function handler and role**. Here, we need to create a new IAM role because we don't only need permission, and S3 not only needs permission to invoke the Lambda function, but the Lambda function also needs permission to retrieve information or to perform the get object request here on S3. So, we need to give that role a name; here, a policy template has been selected already, which is an object read-only permission, because we want to read the content type. Let's call it `PyFunS3Role`:

Scroll down and click **Next**.

Review the configuration and click on **Create function**. Once the function has been created, as shown in the following, let's test it with a synthetic event:

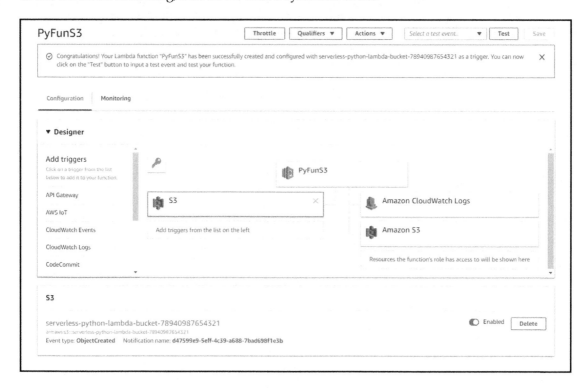

Click on **Actions** | **Configure Test Event**. And, instead of using the Hello World event in the sample event template, let's use an S3 event:

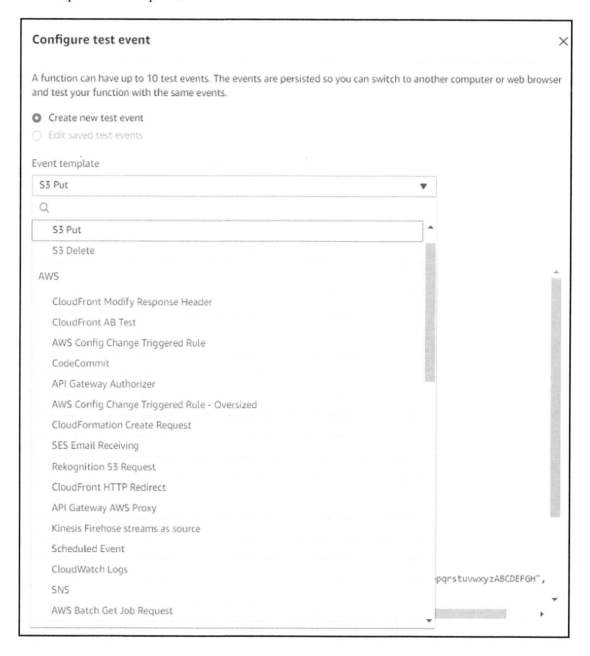

So, this **S3 Put** event should do the trick because it's an object-created event. Click on **Save and Test**.

You can see in the preceding screenshot that we get an access-denied error. Why is that? Actually, we get an error because our `GetObject` operation does not have permission to use the S3 boto client to perform that **GetObject** request. Instead of tweaking the synthetic event, we can also go to our S3 bucket and just invoke the trigger.

Go to the S3 bucket and upload a file. Once it has uploaded, take a look. Go back to the Lambda dashboard, and click on **Monitoring** and **View logs in CloudWatch**:

Here, we can see a log stream, and we can see the **GetObject** operation has failed because access is denied. But we can also see that manually invoking the S3-object-created event has actually worked, and you can see the content type is an image in the following format:

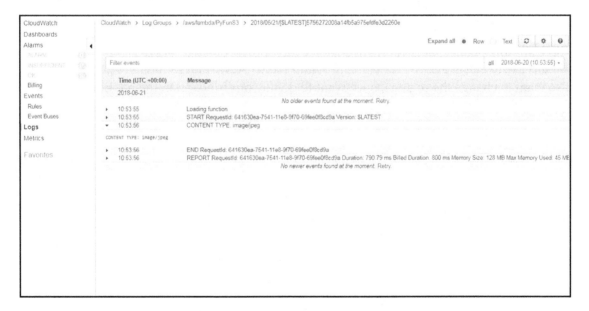

Using the Serverless Framework with Python

In the previous section, we created our first Python Lambda functions on the AWS Management Console. In this section, we will use the serverless framework to create Python Lambda functions. We will invoke the function locally, and then we will deploy and remotely invoke the function.

Open a terminal window in the Atom Editor. We will use the serverless command-line interface to generate a Python Lambda function from the template. If you don't have the serverless framework installed on your computer, please head back to the install and setup video right at the beginning. You should be able to execute this command to print out the serverless version that you have installed. Currently, we're using serverless framework version 1.6.1. You can create a new function using the command, `sls create` and specifying the template, `--template` or, for short, `-t`. Then set the runtime platform, set the language by using `aws-python`, and giving the function the name `pyblog`, as shown here:

```
sls create -t aws-python -n pyblog
```

This will generate some boilerplate code, which can be seen on the left-hand side with the `serverless.yml` file and a `handler.py` file that implement the Lambda function handler. Let's take a look at the `serverless.yml` file first.

There are some boilerplate comment codes, which can be deleted. There is then the name of the service, which is `pyblog` here; the provider name, AWS; and Python version 2.7. We also want to change the region, as we want to deploy our function in the `eu-central-1` `region` in Frankfurt:

```
service: pyblog
provider:
    name: aws
    runtime: python2.7
    stage: dev
    region: eu-central-1
```

Following this, you can also see the reference to the Lambda function:

```
functions:
    hello:
        handler: handler.hello
```

The Lambda function currently has the name `hello`. And it references the function handler, the handler (the `handler.py` file), and the `hello` function in the `py` file, which is shown here:

```python
import json
def hello(event, context):
    body = {
        "message": "Go Serverless v1.0! Your function executed
successfully!",
        "input": event
    }
    response = {
        "statusCode": 200,
        "body": json.dumps(body)
    }

    return response
```

If we invoke this Lambda function with an event, it simply prepares a body with a message property and an input property; in the input property, it just prints out the event that it has been invoked with and then it prepares a response. The body is dumped into JSON and then it returns the response.

You can locally invoke our Lambda function via `sls invoke local`, and then get the function name with `-f`. Right now, the function name is `hello`:

```
Serverless: Successfully generated boilerplate for template: "aws-python"
Admin@Admin:~/Desktop/admin/serverless/programming-aws-lambda-master/python$ sls invoke local -f hello
{
    "body": "{\"input\": {}, \"message\": \"Go Serverless v1.0! Your function executed successfully!\"}",
    "statusCode": 200
}
```

As you can see in the preceding screenshot, it has worked. Hence, we can locally invoke our Lambda function. Let's deploy our Lambda function:

```
Admin@Admin:~/Desktop/admin/serverless/programming-aws-lambda-master/python$ sls deploy
Serverless: Packaging service...
Serverless: Excluding development dependencies...
Serverless: Creating Stack...
Serverless: Checking Stack create progress...
.....
Serverless: Stack create finished...
Serverless: Uploading CloudFormation file to S3...
Serverless: Uploading artifacts...
Serverless: Uploading service .zip file to S3 (12.49 KB)...
Serverless: Validating template...
Serverless: Updating Stack...
Serverless: Checking Stack update progress...
.............
Serverless: Stack update finished...
Service Information
service: pyblog
stage: dev
region: eu-central-1
stack: pyblog-dev
api keys:
  None
endpoints:
  None
functions:
  hello: pyblog-dev-hello
```

Let's now invoke it remotely. You can simply use the command from before, but instead of using `sls invoke local`, we use `sls invoke -f hello`:

```
functions:
  hello: pyblog-dev-hello
Admin@Admin:~/Desktop/admin/serverless/programming-aws-lambda-master/python$ sls invoke -f hello
{
    "body": "{\"input\": {}, \"message\": \"Go Serverless v1.0! Your function executed successfully!\"}",
    "statusCode": 200
}
```

This invokes our remote Lambda function.

In the next section, we are going to build a serverless backend, which is similar to the backend that we built previously with Node.js, but this time we are going to build it with Python.

Building a Serverless backend with Python

In the previous section, we created a simple Lambda function using the serverless framework and Python. Now we will create a more complex service similar to the one that we created using Node.js, but using Python. In this section, we will refactor the Lambda function from our previous section. We will add DynamoDB for data persistence, create the other CRUD operations, and test our deployed service using Postman.

Go back to the Atom Editor where we last left off. Let's refactor the handler function a little bit. For example, we're going to replace the body with a short message, Created new article.

Let's print out the event that the Lambda function has been invoked with. Instead of naming the function handler `hello`, we simply rename it `handler`:

```python
def handler(event, context):
    print('received event{}'.format(event))
    body = {
        "message": "Created new article"
    }

    response = {
        "statusCode": 200,
        "body": json.dumps(body)
    }

    return response
```

Now go to the `serverless.yml` file and rename the file from `hello` to `handler`. It becomes `handler.handle`, but that sounds weird, so we change the name of the `handler.py` file from handler to create, and then go back to the `serverless.yml` and call `hello` to `create` it, as shown here:

```yaml
functions:
  create:
    handler: create.hello
```

Next, we need to give the Lambda function an IAM role that enables it to perform certain DynamoDB operations. So, we replace the commented code with the following IAM role statements:

```yaml
provider:
  name: aws
  runtime: python2.7
  stage: dev
```

```
    region: eu-central-1
    iamRoleStatements:
    - Effect: Allow
      Action:
        - dynamodb:Query
        - dynamodb:GetItem
        - dynamodb:PutItem
        - dynamodb:UpdateItem
        - dynamodb:DeleteItem
      Resource: "arn:aws:dynamodb:eu-
  central-1:186706155491:table/PyBlogTable"
```

Please be aware that the syntax is supposed to change from serverless framework 1.8 upwards, so when that happens, please take a look at the source code in our repository. Do check that out in case it doesn't work with your version of the serverless framework. What we need to do is give the Lambda function permission; that is, allow it to perform certain actions-such as query, get item, put item, and so on-on the resources previously shown. You should replace this with your own resources, so you need to go to the AWS Management Console after your DynamoDB table has been created and make sure that this is the resource. In a moment, we will show you where you find it. After that, scroll down further in the `serverless.yml` file, where we will be able to create additional resources using the CloudFormation resource template, by creating the DynamoDB table that you will give your Lambda function access to, as shown here:

```
resources:
   Resources:
     BlogTable:
        Type: AWS::DynamoDB::Table
        Properties:
          TableName: PyBlogTable
          AttributeDefinitions:
             - AttributeName: article_id
               AttributeType: S
          KeySchema:
             - AttributeName: article_id
               KeyType: HASH
          ProvisionedThroughput:
             ReadCapacityUnits: 1
             WriteCapacityUnits: 1
```

As you can see from the previous screenshot, the table name is `PyBlogTable` and it has one hash key, `article_id`, which is string type. We also specify the capacity units, which is the throughput that is provisioned for the table.

The minimum setting is 1 for read and 1 for write.

The higher the settings, the more throughputs you get, so the more concurrent requests you can make on your DynamoDB table, but also the higher your costs. For our simple application, 1 and 1 are fine. So, once it is set, move over to the function and add an HTTP event. Let's make it a post method instead of a get method because this is a create operation, and, by specifying this here and performing an `sls` a `serverless deploy`, we will also create the appropriate API endpoint using the API Gateway service.

```
functions:
   create:
      handler: create.handler
      events:
        - http:
            path: articles
            method: post
```

Now go to the terminal and do an `sls deploy`, which will result in the following:

```
Admin@Admin:~/Desktop/admin/serverless/programming-aws-lambda-master/python$ sls deploy
Serverless: Packaging service...
Serverless: Excluding development dependencies...
Serverless: Uploading CloudFormation file to S3...
Serverless: Uploading artifacts...
Serverless: Uploading service .zip file to S3 (12.52 KB)...
Serverless: Validating template...
Serverless: Updating Stack...
Serverless: Checking Stack update progress...
.................................
Serverless: Stack update finished...
Service Information
service: pyblog
stage: dev
region: eu-central-1
stack: pyblog-dev
api keys:
  None
endpoints:
  POST - https://jppj97nlo7.execute-api.eu-central-1.amazonaws.com/dev/create
functions:
  create: pyblog-dev-create
```

Once deployed, let's invoke it remotely via `sls invoke` with the function name `create`:

```
functions:
  create: pyblog-dev-create
Admin@Admin:~/Desktop/admin/serverless/programming-aws-lambda-master/python$ sls invoke -f create
{
    "body": "{\"message\": \"Created new article\"}",
    "statusCode": 200
}
```

As you can see in the preceding screenshot, this returns the message `Created new article`. Now let's head over to the AWS Management Console and see if our DynamoDB table has been created. Log into the AWS Management Console and go to the DynamoDB dashboard.

Name	Status	Partition key	Sort key	Indexes	Total read capacity	Total write
BlogTable	Active	article_id (String)	-	0	1	1
PyBlogTable	Active	article_id (String)	-	0	1	1

Viewing 2 of 2 Tables

As you can see, the `PyBlogTable` has, in fact, been created. If you click on it, you will be able to see some additional information. If you scroll down on the **Overview** tab, you can also see the ARN, which is the string that identifies your table as an Amazon resource. So, copy that and paste it into your `serverless.yml` file in the `iamRoleStatements`. The `iamRoleStatements` gives your Lambda function permission to perform the actions on this resource, and this is the resource that specifies your DynamoDB table.

Now we have created a DynamoDB table and our Lambda function has permission to access the table, but, actually, if we take a look at the `create.py` function handler, it doesn't really do anything yet. So, we need to replace the code with the following:

```python
from_future_import print_function #Python 2/3 compatibility
import json
import boto3
import uuid

def handler(event, context):
    print('received create event{}'.format(event))
    dynamodb = boto3.resource('dynamodb', region_name='eu-central-1')
    table = dynamodb.Table('PyBlogTable')
    id = str(uuid.uuid1())

    put_response = table.put_Item(
```

```
        Item = {
            'article_id': id,
            'text': 'hello python'
            }
        }
    print('put response{}'.format(put_response))
```

Here, we are importing the boto library. This is globally installed on the instance that executes your Lambda function, so you don't need to install this dependency. You can simply import it and use it; for example, here it is used to instantiate a DynamoDB client. On the DynamoDB client, we want to access the `PyBlogTable`, and, since we are going to create a new item, we are going to create a UUID; then prepare a `put_item` request with the following item content, which is an `article_id`, with our randomly generated UUID and the following hard-coded text:

```
put_response = table.put_item(
    Item = {
        'article_id': id,
        'text': 'hello python'
        }
    )
```

This will return the following `put_response`, which we are going to print out on the console, and also we're going to play it back in our response, as shown here:

```
print('put response{}'.format(put_response))

response = {
    "statusCode": 200,
    "body": json.dumps(put_response)
}
```

Now we will do an `sls deploy` to update our service and then test if it works:

```
Admin@Admin:~/Desktop/admin/serverless/programming-aws-lambda-master/python$ sls deploy
Serverless: Packaging service...
Serverless: Excluding development dependencies...
Serverless: Uploading CloudFormation file to S3...
Serverless: Uploading artifacts...
Serverless: Uploading service .zip file to S3 (12.69 KB)...
Serverless: Validating template...
Serverless: Updating Stack...
Serverless: Checking Stack update progress...
...............
Serverless: Stack update finished...
Service Information
service: pyblog
stage: dev
region: eu-central-1
stack: pyblog-dev
api keys:
  None
endpoints:
  POST - https://jppj97nlo7.execute-api.eu-central-1.amazonaws.com/dev/create
functions:
  create: pyblog-dev-create
```

Once the service has been deployed, we use a synthetic dummy event to test the Lambda function. Create a new file in your directory. Here, we name the new `event.json` with the following content:

```
{
"body": {\article_id":\"8268c73-fdc7-11e6-8554-985aeb8c9bcc"\,\"text\":
\"Hello Universe\"}"
}
```

We then perform an `sls invoke` with the create function and specify the path to the
`event.json` file:

```
Admin@Admin:~/Desktop/admin/serverless/programming-aws-lambda-master/python$ sls invoke -f create -p event.json
{
    "body": "{\"ResponseMetadata\": {\"RetryAttempts\": 0, \"HTTPStatusCode\": 200, \"RequestId\": \"742VSAUSNUQG0JFELD073VHM4RVV4KQNS05AEMVJF66Q9AS
UAAJG\", \"HTTPHeaders\": {\"x-amzn-requestid\": \"742VSAUSNUQG0JFELD073VHM4RVV4KQNS05AEMVJF66Q9ASUAAJG\", \"content-length\": \"2\", \"server\": \"
Server\", \"connection\": \"keep-alive\", \"x-amz-crc32\": \"2745614147\", \"date\": \"Sat, 23 Jun 2018 07:16:07 GMT\", \"content-type\": \"applicat
ion/x-amz-json-1.0\"}}}",
    "statusCode": 200
}
```

After invoking this, we head back to our AWS Management Console and go to the
DynamoDB dashboard. Have a look in the **Items** tab:

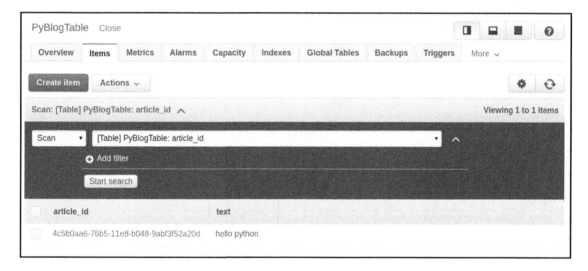

Our hello python article has been created. Copy the read, update, and delete Python Lambda function handlers into the directory, and update the `serverless.yml` file. We also need to change the path a little bit, so, instead of `createnow`, it says `articles`. For the read article, we give it a path parameter, which is the ID of my article as shown here:

```
functions:
    create:
        handler: create.handler
        events:
            - http:
                path: articles
                method: post
    read:
        handler: read.handler
        events:
            - http:
                path: articles/{id}
                method: get
    update:
        handler: update.handler
        events:
```

We can perform put operations to update the article and can also perform delete operations to delete articles:

```
update:
    handler: update.handler
    events:
        - http:
            path: articles
            method: put
delete:
    handler: delete.handler
    events:
        - http:
            path: articles
            method: delete
```

The rest is the same as before. We also need to add respective function handlers to get items from the DynamoDB table, return them in response to the update articles in the DynamoDB table, and delete articles in the DynamoDB table. We also need to add a path parameter to the event.json file, so that we can test the read-article function handler, as shown here:

```
{
  "pathParameters": {"article_id": "d4b8d9f0-fdc6-11e6-9cc5-985aeb8c9bcc"},
  "body": "{\"article_id\":\"82682c73-fdc7-11e6-8554-985aeb8c9bcc\",
\"text\": \"Hello World\"}"
}
```

Now deploy the function and test the API using Postman. To test the API, copy the following endpoint, then open Postman and use the endpoint:

```
Admin@Admin:~/Desktop/admin/serverless/programming-aws-lambda-master/python$ sls deploy
Serverless: Packaging service...
Serverless: Excluding development dependencies...
Serverless: Uploading CloudFormation file to S3...
Serverless: Uploading artifacts...
Serverless: Uploading service .zip file to S3 (14.27 KB)...
Serverless: Validating template...
Serverless: Updating Stack...
Serverless: Checking Stack update progress...
..............................................................................
Serverless: Stack update finished...
Service Information
service: pyblog
stage: dev
region: eu-central-1
stack: pyblog-dev
api keys:
  None
endpoints:
  POST - https://jppj97nlo7.execute-api.eu-central-1.amazonaws.com/dev/articles
  GET - https://jppj97nlo7.execute-api.eu-central-1.amazonaws.com/dev/articles/{id}
  PUT - https://jppj97nlo7.execute-api.eu-central-1.amazonaws.com/dev/articles
  DELETE - https://jppj97nlo7.execute-api.eu-central-1.amazonaws.com/dev/articles
functions:
  create: pyblog-dev-create
  read: pyblog-dev-read
  update: pyblog-dev-update
  delete: pyblog-dev-delete
```

Open Postman and select the post HTTP method to create a new article. Paste the endpoint that we copied previously, and add the following JSON file as a payload to post the request, as shown here, and click **Send**:

This will return the `article_id` of the article that has been created. Copy that and perform a get request. This returns the texts that we have just created with our article **Hello from Postman**, as shown here:

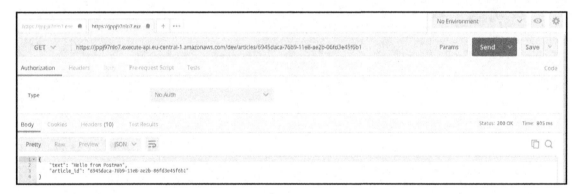

Summary

In this chapter, we learned how to create Lambda functions from blueprints on the AWS Management Console using Python. Then we used the serverless framework with Python to create a slightly more complex service that includes Lambda, API Gateway, and DynamoDB. In the next chapter, we are going to program AWS Lambda using C#.

6
Programming AWS Lambda with C#

At the time of working on this chapter, C# is the newest language addition to the AWS platform. You can now build Lambda functions and serverless applications using C# and .NET tools. In this chapter, we are going to cover the following topics:

- Creating C# Lambda functions with .NET Core
- Creating C# serverless projects with .NET Core

Creating C# Lambda functions with .NETCore

In this section, we are going to create a Lambda function using .NET Core. We are going to take a look at how to install the AWS Toolkit for Visual Studio. Then, we are going to try out some features of the AWS Toolkit and we'll use it to create our first C# Lambda function.

Firstly, we need to download the AWS Toolkit for Visual Studio, so download and execute the installer, and launch Visual Studio. After you have signed up for an AWS account, sign in to the AWS Management Console. Click on **Services** in the upper left-hand corner and select **IAM**, which will navigate you to the **Identity and Access Management** dashboard:

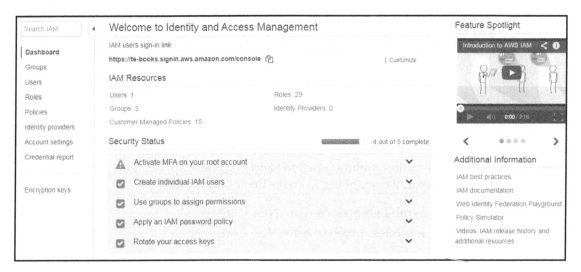

Now, we need to create a special user with permissions to access AWS services programmatically. This allows us to set up our local development environment in a way that IDEs' development frameworks can use AWS on our behalf. You should set up an **IAM** user to keep your AWS account secure because you can simply create an IAM user with a set of permissions and, after performing the exercises using that IAM user, you can later delete it. Therefore, your access credentials are not prone to the risk of being abused by somebody else if another person gets access to your identity and access. Here, let's create a special user for the purpose of this chapter. We are going to give this user access permissions to use AWS services programmatically. It's always good practice to create an IAM user with specially tailored permissions. For the purpose of this tutorial, let's create a user to access AWS services on our behalf; for example, from the Eclipse IDE or through the serverless framework. After you have performed the exercise in this tutorial, you can simply delete this IAM user, so you won't run the risk of accidentally exposing your credentials in a way that somebody else can use your AWS account on your behalf.

First, we're going to create an IAM group, so click on **Groups** on the left-hand side. Create a new group named `learninggroup` and click on **Next Step**. For simplicity, give the group administrator access. This is not the best security guideline, but it's simple and gets us started quickly. You can, and you should, probably delete this group as soon as you are done with performing these exercises. Click on **Next Step** and the group is created.

Now we need to assign the user to the newly created group. Go back to the dashboard, create a user, and assign the user to the newly created group. Click on the **Add User** button and give the user the name `learninglambda`. Also, give the user programmatic access. This will create an access key ID and a secret access key for your user, so the command-line interface, serverless framework, SDK or other development tools that are set up on your local computer can access AWS services on your behalf. Click on the **Next Permissions** button.

So far, we have added a user to the group `learninggroup` and now we are going to create the user. Once our user has been created successfully, it creates an access key ID and secret access key for your user. Copy this information into a text editor for now.

Creating an AWS Lambda project

Let's get started by creating a new AWS Lambda project.

1. Click on **File** | **New** | **Project**.

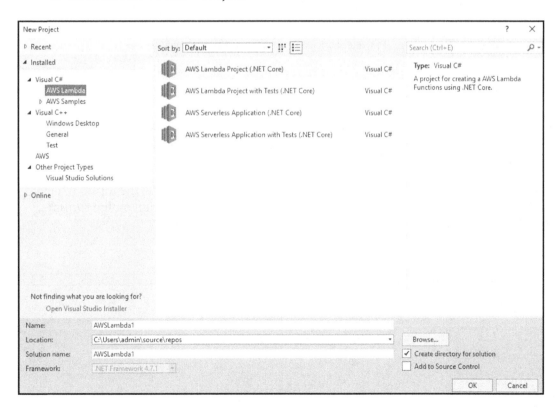

To install the AWS Toolkit, you should see the preceding options on the left-hand side, including AWS Lambda, and there are some sample projects with sample code for your reference.

2. Let's get started with a very simple **AWS Lambda Project** using the **.NETCore** framework. Leave the defaults as they are, as AWSLambda1, and click **OK**.
3. Select one of the blueprints. Let's get started with a really simple empty function blueprint. Click **Finish**.

Our AWS Lambda project has been created and it will show up in our **Solution Explorer**. Now let's take a look at the function handler:

So, from the preceding screenshot, the structure of the Lambda function looks similar to the examples that we have seen before for Java and other programming languages. We have our function handler, and the function handler takes two arguments: the input, which in this case is a string, and the context object, which gives us information on the runtime context of our Lambda function.

```
public string FunctionHandler(string input, ILambdaContext context)
{
    return input?.ToUpper();
}
```

This Lambda function simply takes the input, transforms it into uppercase characters, and returns them. Also, make sure that you are in the right region. Here, we are deploying our Lambda function into the EU Central region and Frankfurt. Give our function the name CSFunction, and click **Next**, which will lead you to select some further configurations for our Lambda function, such as an IAM role. For example, if you want to access other AWS services from within your Lambda function, you need to select an IAM role that gives your Lambda function permission to do that. We can also configure the amount of memory. For now, select the smallest amount. We also select the timeout, which is the time after which our function will time out, as shown here:

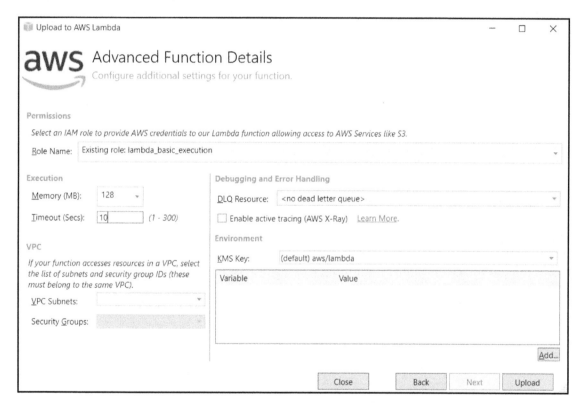

For the IAM role, we simply choose the Lambda basic execution role, as shown in the previous screenshot, which has no special permissions. Click on **Upload** to upload the Lambda function.

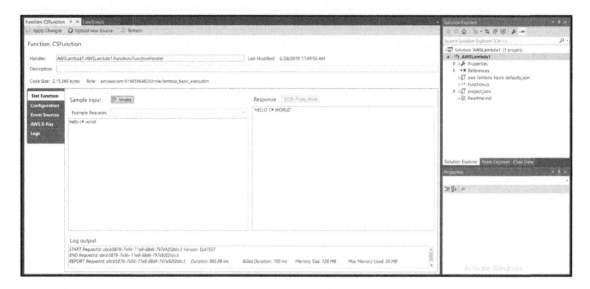

As you can see from the previous screenshot, we have created our first Lambda function with C#. If we give it some input and invoke it, we get our uppercase string as return. Head to the AWS Management Console and have a look at our Lambda function there. On the AWS Lambda dashboard, you can see that four functions have been created: for getting all blogs, for getting a single blog, for adding a blog, and for removing a blog. This is as follows:

Function name	▼	Description	Runtime	▼	Code size	▼	Last Modified	▼
○ cs-serverless-stack-AddBlog-16BU9MMEDDA8S		Function to get add a blog	C# (.NET Core 1.0)		577.8 kB		in 5 hours	
○ cs-serverless-stack-GetBlogs-MLXIN1Z5SA1E		Function to get a list of blogs	C# (.NET Core 1.0)		577.8 kB		in 5 hours	
○ cs-serverless-stack-GetBlog-FORJYMRGX2ZX		Function to get a single blog	C# (.NET Core 1.0)		577.8 kB		in 5 hours	
○ cs-serverless-stack-RemoveBlog-IASTKIJXJH01		Function to remove a blog	C# (.NET Core 1.0)		577.8 kB		in 5 hours	

Head over to the DynamoDB dashboard. A new table, **CsBlogTable**, has been created. It has a single hash ID or primary partition key, with name Id and type string:

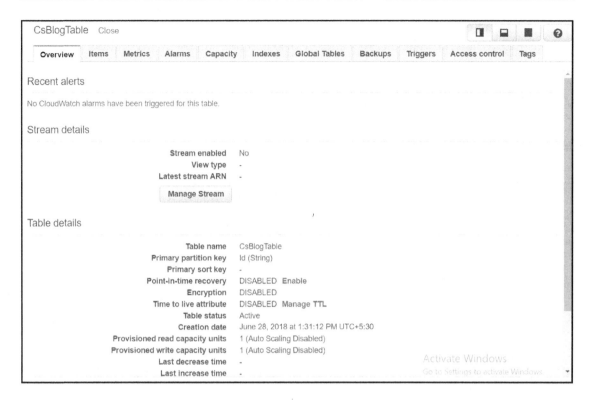

Let's try out our API by invoking it with Postman. Go back to Visual Studio and log into the AWS Management Console. We've deployed all our functions in the Frankfurt region. As you can see here, we have a new addition, the **CSFunction**:

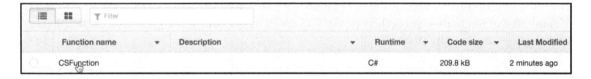

You can take a look at it by clicking on **Monitoring**. As you can see in the following screenshot, we have just had an error and we also had one successful invocation:

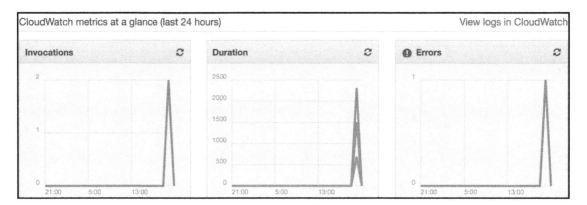

If you click on **CloudWatch**, you can also view the logs there that you have just seen in your Visual Studio log console. Next, we are going to create a serverless application with C# and the .NET Core framework.

Creating C# Serverless Project with .NET Core

In the previous section, we used Visual Studio and the AWS Toolkit to create our first AWS Lambda function with C#. Now we will create a more complex serverless project that contains Lambda functions and the API Gateway. We are going to use the AWS Toolkit and Visual Studio to create a serverless project. We will also explore the generated source code and deploy and test the project.

1. Go to Visual Studio 2015 and create a new serverless project. Select **File | New | Project**.
2. Select **AWS Serverless Application** and click **OK**.
3. We are creating a little bit more complex application, so select the **Blog API using DynamoDB**.

4. Our serverless project has been created. There are two files that have been generated for us, `Blog.cs` file and `Functions.cs` file, as shown here:

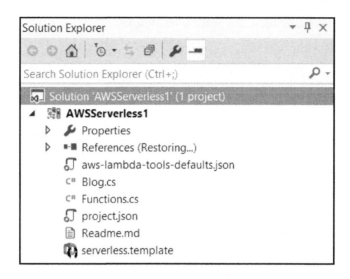

In the `Functions.cs` file, we find the function handlers that are used to implement the business logic for our Blog API. First, there is a constructor that sets up the context for our DynamoDB:

```
namespace AWSServerless1
{
    public class Functions
    {
        const string TABLENAME_ENVIRONMENT_VARIABLE_LOOKUP = "BlogTable";

        public const string ID_QUERY_STRING_NAME = " Id";
        IDynamoDBContext DDBContext {get; set; }
        public Functions()
        {
            var tablename =
System.Environment.GetEnvironmentVariable(TABLENAME_ENVIRONMENT_VARIABLE_LO
OKUP);
            if(!string.IsNullOrEmpty(tableName))
            {
                AWSConfigDynamoDB.COntext.TypeMappings[typeof(Blog)] = new
                Amazon.Util.TypeMapping(typeof(BlogTable))
            }
            var config = new DynamoDBContextConfig {COnversion =
DynamoDBEntryConversion.V2};
```

For example, in the previous screenshot, we retrieve the table name from an environment variable and set up the context for our DynamoDB client. Following this, you will see the main business functions, such as get blogs. You can also retrieve a blog identified by its blog ID. We read the blog ID from the path parameters:

```
public async Task<APIGatewayProxyResponse>
GetBlogAsync(APIGatewayProxyRequest request, ILambdaContext)
{
    string blogId = null;
    if(request.PathParameters != null &&
request.PathParameters.ContainsKey(ID_QUERY_STRING_NAME))
        blogId = request.PathParameters[ID_QUERY-STRING_NAME];
    else if(request.QueryStringParameters[ID-QUERY-STRING_NAME]);
```

Further to this, we use the DynamoDB client to retrieve the blog from our DynamoDB table:

```
context.Logger.LogLine($"Getting blog (blogId}");
var blog = await DDBContext.LoadAsync<Blog>(blogId);
context.Logger.LogLine($"Found blog: {blog!= null}");

if(blog == null)
{
    return new APIGatewayProxyResponse
    {
        StatusCode = (int)HttpStatusCode.NotFound
    };
}
```

In the following screenshot, we are preparing an API Gateway proxy response, so we set the HTTP status code, body, and headers in our code instead of setting these in our AWS Management Console. This is pretty similar to the approach in the serverless framework and Lambda proxy integration.

```
var response = new APIGatewayProxyResponse
{
    StatusCode = (int)HttpStatusCode.OK,
    Body = JsonConvert.SerializeObject(blog),
    Headers = new Dictionary<string, string>{{"Content-Type",
"application/json"}}
};
return response;
```

In addition, we have a function that adds the blog post and a function for removing a blog post.

In our **Solution Explorer**, we can see the `serverless.template`, which contains the serverless application model, as shown here:

```
{
    "AWSTemplateFormatVersion": "2010-09-09",
    "Transform": "AWS::Serverless-2016-10-31",
    "Description": "AWS Serverless API that exposes the add, remove and get
operations for a blogging
    platform"
    "Parameters": {
      "ShouldCreateTable"
```

This is basically an extension of the CloudFormation syntax that we use it to create AWS resources. For example, we specify the Lambda functions to get blogs, get a single blog identified by its ID, add blogs, and remove blogs. We also specify the blog table that is being created in DynamoDB.

Let's try it out. Right-click on the **AWS Serverless1** in the **Solution Explorer**, and **Publish to AWS Lambda**; we can use the same account settings as before, as shown in the following:

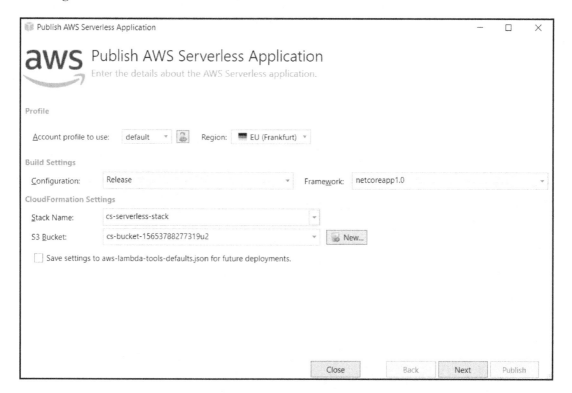

Select the stack name and create a new bucket to which our CloudFormation code will be uploaded. Click **Next**.

We then need to enter the environment variables that will be used in our function code, as you have seen before. We also need to enter a table name for the blog table that is being created in DynamoDB. We call it `CsBlogTable`, as shown here:

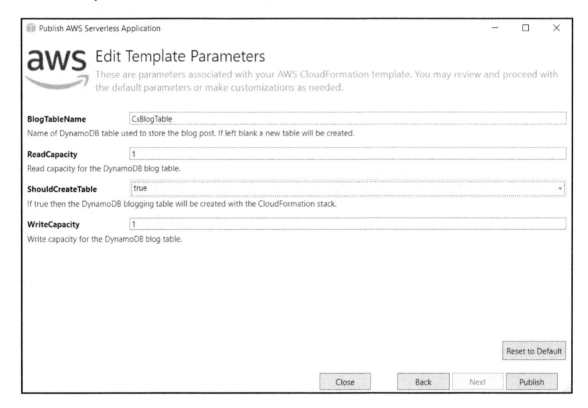

The minimum settings for reading capacity and write capacity for DynamoDB are 1 and 1. Once that is done, click on **Publish**.

You will be able to see the current **Status** of the CloudFormation stack that will create our resources, which should end with `Create_Completed`.

 If there was an error in your setup, you should get some info back on your console. Or you can go to the AWS Management Console dashboard, then head over to the CloudFormation dashboard, and see what has gone wrong. You can also delete your CloudFormations stack and all the resources that have been created here by going to your AWS Management Console and simply deleting the stack.

You can also go to the AWS Management dashboard and take a look what has been created.

Just copy the URL to our API and open Postman.

Summary

We have explored programming Lambda using Java, Python, and C#. In the case of Java, we used Eclipse with the AWS Toolkit plugin to create simple Lambda functions, as well as more complex serverless projects that include multiple Lambda functions, the API Gateway service, and DynamoDB. Similarly, in the case of C#, we used Visual Studio with the AWS Toolkit to create simple Lambda functions, as well as a more complex serverless project. For Python, we used the serverless framework.

Other Books You May Enjoy

If you enjoyed this book, you may be interested in these other books by Packt:

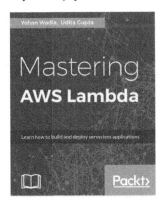

Mastering AWS Lambda
Yohan Wadia, Udita Gupta

ISBN: 978-1-78646-769-0

- Understand the hype, significance, and business benefits of Serverless computing and applications
- Plunge into the Serverless world of AWS Lambda and master its core components and how it works
- Find out how to effectively and efficiently design, develop, and test Lambda functions using Node.js, along with some keen coding insights and best practices
- Explore best practices to effectively monitor and troubleshoot Serverless applications using AWS CloudWatch and other third-party services in the form of Datadog and Loggly
- Quickly design and develop Serverless applications by leveraging AWS Lambda, DynamoDB, and API Gateway using the Serverless Application Framework (SAF) and other AWS services such as Step Functions
- Explore a rich variety of real-world Serverless use cases with Lambda and see how you can apply it to your environments

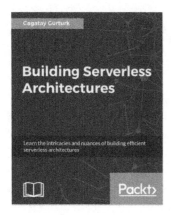

Building Serverless Architectures
Cagatay Gurturk

ISBN: 978-1-78712-919-1

- Learn to form microservices from bigger Softwares
- Orchestrate and scale microservices
- Design and set up the data flow between cloud services and custom business logic
- Get to grips with cloud provider's APIs, limitations, and known issues
- Migrate existing Java applications to a serverless architecture
- Acquire deployment strategies
- Build a highly available and scalable data persistence layer
- Unravel cost optimization techniques

Leave a review - let other readers know what you think

Please share your thoughts on this book with others by leaving a review on the site that you bought it from. If you purchased the book from Amazon, please leave us an honest review on this book's Amazon page. This is vital so that other potential readers can see and use your unbiased opinion to make purchasing decisions, we can understand what our customers think about our products, and our authors can see your feedback on the title that they have worked with Packt to create. It will only take a few minutes of your time, but is valuable to other potential customers, our authors, and Packt. Thank you!

Index